RECIPROCAL MISSIONS

SHORT-TERM MISSIONS THAT SERVE EVERYONE

By DJ Schuetze and Phil Steiner

P & D Publishing

San Diego, California

DJ Schuetze & Phil Steiner

P&D Publishing

San Diego, CA

www.PandDpublishing.com

Book Layout ©2017BookDesignTemplates.com

Reciprocal Missions / DJ Schuetze and Phil Steiner. —1st ed.

ISBN 978-0-6982-09052-7

*Definition of Reciprocal on the back cover -
http://www.gingersoftware.com/content/grammar-rules/reciprocal-pronouns/*

Contents

"Without genuine relationships with the poor, we rob them of their dignity, and they become mere projects. And God didn't intend for anyone to become our projects."

— Eugene Cho

Our Story

Short-term missions, when healthy, can change the lives of everyone involved. When done wrong, real damage can occur; or at the very least, efforts can be a waste of time and resources. How do we remedy this?

Many books have deconstructed short-term missions and have, sadly, caused people to stop participating in these life-changing trips. But we don't want people to give up short-term missions. There is something God does in the hearts and lives of His people when they step out of their comfort zone, travel to a new place, and spend time observing and participating in ministry in cultures different from their own.

Just like any effective ministry, in missions relationships are key. Healthy, reciprocal relationships are critical to successful short-term mission trips. Without them we will continue to do damage and be ineffective. The book you're reading is a guide to help you navigate short-term missions in a way that honors everyone: the teams going, the ministries hosting, and the local communities.

You'll notice this book has a slightly different flow than most. One of us will work through a section from our perspective—a topic in our particular area of expertise; then the other will briefly chime in, sharing their short take on the topic. DJ writes from the perspective of the mission host; he has received and hosted groups for over 25 years. Phil writes from the perspective of the short-term trip facilitator, bringing 20 years of experience leading groups in effective service and educational experiences. The dialogue that results provides insights into best practices for healthy short-term missions.

After spending years working to create a healthier approach to short term missions, both of us have learned firsthand the power of building solid ministry partnerships. We know from personal experience the blessings and benefits when missions are done in a healthy, humble, reciprocal way. This process wasn't always easy or straightforward for either of us, but through honest dialogue and consistent commitment to high quality short-term missions, we are now able to share our lessons learned with you.

.

DJ's Story

Many people have a defining moment in their life. Whether positive or negative, it is branded into their memory and will be with them until they die. My defining moment came through short-term missions.

I get asked almost daily about how I was first called into orphan care. I can still remember the sights, smells, and emotions during that day that changed my life 25 years ago. The defining moment that would radically shift the direction of my life happened to be shared with someone who I had never met before, during their defining moment. Our lives would be forever changed in a few hours together, and we would never see each other again.

I was comfortable in my life as a successful Christian businessman, helping with the high school group at my church in my spare time. I assumed that would be the direction of my life and had no problem with that. I was comfortable; I wasn't even considering that God might have something else in mind. I had been helping lead our church high school group on short-term mission trips to serve a very small, very depressing orphanage in northern Baja, Mexico. I enjoyed serving the kids in the orphanage, but I also loved the change I was seeing in my high school students as they learned to serve others. Unbeknownst to me, God was making similar changes in my heart.

One day I got a call from the orphanage. They needed something brought down from the U.S. and asked if I could help. I had a Saturday open and offered to drive down. While I was there, a 10-year-old boy was being dropped off. Most people don't think about it, but every child in an orphanage has a first day. Almost always it is a terrifying, horrible experience they will remember for the rest of their lives. They have either been abandoned by their family or removed due to abuse or neglect. To them the reasons are irrelevant—everything they've ever known is gone, and they've landed in a scary building, crowded with strangers.

As I watched this boy being dropped off, I could see how scared he was. I didn't speak the language at the time, but even if I did, what do you say to that? What did I have to offer that child when he was at his most fragile point? I couldn't tell him it was going to be OK (I didn't know if that were true); I couldn't tell him he landed in a good orphanage (he didn't); everything I had in my youth ministry bag of tricks was useless. So I sat with him. We split a Coke. He cried. And a couple of hours later I got in my car and drove home.

I hurt for that child, I hurt for that child deeply, but intertwined with the hurt was something I had never experienced before. I had been involved in a lot of ministries, but I've never felt so used by God as sitting with that boy, in the dirt, at that moment, when he desperately needed somebody. I wanted more of that in my life. I wanted to experience more of being used by God to touch and serve people at that level. Everything I had been working toward suddenly became incredibly trivial and pointless in comparison to those few hours in Baja. That was the day I knew I wanted to shift my path from where I was headed, into something more profound. For almost 25 years now, I have worked full-time in orphan care and facilitating short-term mission trips.

It's impossible to plan a defining moment in your life, but if we step out of our comfort zone and place ourselves in new and challenging circumstances, those defining moments are more likely to happen. We won't know what a prison ministry, a homeless ministry, or the powerful ministry of encouraging others is like until we're willing to take that first step and put ourselves in uncomfortable and awkward situations.

In my experience, both personally and as a witness to thousands of others, few activities encourage more defining moments than short-term missions. There's something about leaving your home country, crossing borders, and making yourself available to be used by God in new circumstances. Short-term missions, when done right, can bring a heightened sense of awareness and help to bring our priorities in line. Although people might be on a mission to share the Gospel and meet the needs of others, there is frequently a whole deeper layer of ministry going on where God is working on us.

Over the years I've received countless letters, emails, and comments from people sharing with me how a short-term mission trip to our orphanage changed their lives. I know many people today who are in full-time ministry as a direct result of a defining moment brought about through short-term missions. For countless others who aren't in full-time ministry, a short-term mission trip becomes an experience that will ripple out in their lives for years to come. It can become a touchstone that they will remember forever.

Phil and I met through short-term missions and his desire to not only bring groups to Mexico, but his desire to bring groups and do it correctly. I've seen him bring hundreds of groups to Mexico and help them experience their own defining moments. In recent years, along with working together in Mexico, we've been traveling together to serve in Ghana, West Africa where we see God's work continuing. We've seen, and continue to see, reciprocal missions change lives for all those involved.

Reciprocal Missions

Phil's Story

For me, it wasn't so much a defining moment but a series of small moments that God used to call me into the work I am doing now. In 1990, while in high school, I went on my first short-term mission trip to a church camp in the mountains of Arizona where I was a counselor for kids from inner city Phoenix. The following year we went to Spain to work at a Bible Institute in Barcelona. I have never felt so used by God as I did on these trips. Fast forward a couple of years and I had the opportunity to co-lead trips to Appalachia and Nicaragua for high school students while working for a parachurch ministry. These experiences not only changed the lives of the students, but they changed my life as well—I wanted more!

In 2006, out of a heart and passion for others to experience God like I had, I led a spring break trip of 19 high school students and 5 adults to Door of Faith Orphanage in La Mision, Mexico. The trip was a great success. This is where I met DJ Schuetze, the American leader of the orphanage. I was deeply impacted by the vision and mission of Door of Faith, as well as DJ's heart for serving and loving others, especially those on the underside of life. It was this first trip where our friendship began. The following spring break I led another trip, this time with over 40 high school students. The popularity of the trip continued to grow and more students, adults, schools and churches wanted to experience this powerful transformative trip.

As we continued to facilitate these trips, we made many mistakes, and I'm sure did damage in the community in which we were serving. Many of our mistakes were because we just didn't know what we didn't know. By God's grace He began to reveal to me what changes needed to be made.

I began to sense an uneasiness about how we were doing these trips. I knew that what we were doing wasn't quite right, and we needed to change our approach. Over the course of the next few years of going to the same community and orphanage several times a year, I began to realize and learn what our presence and impact was having on the orphanage and community, and it wasn't always as positive and effective as I thought it was. I also began to realize that there were a lot of false assumptions I had about the people we were serving with in Mexico. Our actions and words were communicating something that wasn't dignifying and honoring to everyone. My motivation for doing these short-term mission trips wasn't always pure. Though we were building houses, dorms, and repairing roofs, we weren't building what many of these people wanted most—relationship.

Over the course of the next few years I allowed myself to be led by people who lived in Mexico, like DJ, to help me more fully understand the nuances and the impact short-term mission trips have in the community in which we go to serve. I listened to their stories of what groups had done well and the disasters that other groups caused. We built relationships with the indigenous leaders with a desire to understand how we could most effectively and lovingly serve together. It has been through long-term reciprocal, humble relationships with DJ and others that I have learned how to lead these trips to honor and serve everyone. Though not perfect, and I do not have it all figured out, I believe that we can continue to do the hard work of building relationships and furthering the Kingdom of God together when we build reciprocal relationships that serve everyone.

Over the course of the last 18 years we have facilitated short-term mission trips for over 2,000 students and adults, while expanding our long-term partners to San Francisco Bay Area and Ghana, West Africa. Then in spring of 2017 my family and I moved to Mexico to work more closely with the communities we are serving, as well as to more effectively facilitate short-term mission trips. Though we still make mistakes, we are growing and learning. Leading short-term mission trips has been one of my deepest joys, as I have met some of the most amazing men and women who have given their lives for the sake of the Gospel and amazing students and adults who have a desire to love and serve their neighbors. The greatest impact we can have on our short-term mission trips is through long-term humble reciprocal relationships. It is a lot of hard work and commitment, but if we are about furthering the Kingdom of God and honoring everyone involved, it is well worth the effort.

The two of us have known each other over a decade. A little over a year ago we began to dream about writing a book that could provide a new and different way forward for short-term mission trips. We had read all the books that seemed to bash short-term missions. Much of what was being said was true, but we believed that there was a different way to do these trips.

Through our relationship and experience in leading and hosting short-term mission groups, we have seen with our own eyes the power of building solid ministry partnerships—partnerships where trust is built over time and the relationship is mutually beneficial and edifying for all those involved. We know the blessings and benefits when missions are done in a healthy, humble, reciprocal way.

The Kingdom of God is longer, wider, and deeper than any of us can fully comprehend. Getting out of our routine for a week or two and spending time in another culture is one step toward a greater understanding of God's love for all people. It's important to continue to provide that opportunity for people to see God at work in cultures that are not their own. The key is, we need to approach short-term missions in a way that serves everyone. Let's walk together through how we can do short-term missions correctly and in a life changing way.

CHAPTER 1

Short-Term Missions Must Be Reciprocal

DJ

The church in America is an interesting animal. Over the years it has done some incredibly positive work, and at the same time, if we are honest, the church has done a lot of damage—much as our predecessors have done around the world for centuries. One ongoing and problematic issue of the church—it tends to have a pack mentality. Whether it's calling for the prohibition of alcohol one hundred years ago, the rabid opposition to secular music about 30 years ago, or the spike in end-time studies that seem to come around every 10 or 15 years, the church follows trends.

One of the current trends in the church (besides opening coffee houses and using pallets for decoration *everywhere*) is to question the value of short-term missions. Why spend so much money sending a team so far? Aren't mission teams stealing jobs that locals should be doing? What can a group of high school kids do? Aren't we doing more harm than good?

Missions have been a double-edged sword through most of church history. There is a lot to question and a lot of mistakes to repent of and avoid in the future—but there is also a great deal of positive when missions are done right. Missions have done a tremendous amount of good, and some deep damage, but missions are an important part of our faith. We have our orders in the Gospel of Mark: "Go into all the world and preach the Gospel to all creation" (Mark 16:15).

We have a responsibility and a calling to serve others. It's critical to take an honest look at missions and approach them correctly, lovingly, and with a humble heart. This book is about how to do just that, particularly on short-term mission trips.

At the crux of the issue with missions, long-term or short-term, is that any ministry inherently involves people. People are messy. By definition anything people are involved in will eventually become messy and complicated; short-term missions are no different. Anyone who has been involved with a church knows all too well that people are broken and tend to create a great deal of drama, even in the healthiest of situations. But that doesn't mean the church should not work with them or that it's healthy to abandon them. Just like the church, short-term missions have hurt people, and they should be done better, but past mistakes and ongoing complications are not a good reason to abandon the practice of short-term missions. Instead, we have to dig deeper, we have to learn to love better, we have to develop reciprocal relationships that benefit everyone involved.

Marriage as an Analogy for Missions

If one looks at marriage as an institution and judges it on the end results, it would be very easy to mount an argument for abolishing it. Marriage is messy. Marriage is difficult. A healthy marriage is complicated, requiring ongoing effort. Frequently, marriages require outside counsel and guidance. Way too many marriages ultimately end badly. Too often there is intentional or even unintentional abuse. All that being said, very few people in the church would say the institution of marriage should come to an end. When both parties are serving with humility, understanding, and a desire to build each other up, the institution of marriage can be a spectacular gift from God. If people enter into marriage with selfish motivations or unrealistic expectations, a healthy marriage is incredibly difficult, if not impossible. How we prepare and enter into marriage sets the foundation for a healthy loving endeavor, and God is glorified.

Reread the last paragraph, switching "marriage" to "short-term missions." Short-term missions are messy, can cause deep harm, and require a great deal of effort. All these things are accurate. But when it does work well, short-term missions, like marriage, can be an incredible gift from God that changes the lives of those involved for the better. It is worth all the effort.

Often when a marriage ends in divorce, it's usually the result of unmet expectations: "I thought marriage would solve my loneliness." "I thought you would be a better homemaker." "I thought you would be a better provider." When people go on short-term missions with unrealistic expectations, a similar thing happens—disappointment and discouragement. The trip may be seen as a failure. In a short-term mission trip, set realistic goals and expectations—and communicate them to everyone involved. At the same time, flexibility is vital because it's rare that our expectations line up with what God has planned.

Just like in marriage, how we respond when things don't go as planned is critical. If you expect things to be perfect, then you're going to be disappointed. Managing our expectations is healthy and critical for our own well-being. When a trip doesn't go according to plan, we have a simple choice: we can become frustrated with the difficulties, or we can flow with it and enjoy the mess. God sees a much grander panorama, and ultimately, even with apt planning, very little of what goes on is in our control anyway.

DJ Schuetze & Phil Steiner

A Narrow Perspective Causes Harm

Often our simplistic perspective causes the messiness of short-term missions. Many Americans pass judgment on short-term missions from the comfortable position of sitting in the U.S. and judging from afar, without adequate understanding of other cultural contexts. It's important to look at difficult, complicated, multilevel situations from many perspectives.

A few years ago a member of my American staff here in Mexico was very vocal about how terrible all the new factories in Mexico were because they were abusing the workers and taking advantage of the low wages in Mexico. After she had rambled on for a while, a good friend of mine, who was raised and educated in Mexico and is familiar with the factory systems, walked in. As neutrally as I could, I asked him, "What's your feeling on the factory programs?" His immediate response was, "Send more." He explained that the factories were providing much-needed jobs, at a higher pay scale than had been seen in generations. Yes, the workers are making less than their American counterparts, but they are making more than any of their peers. Perspective is needed before we pass judgment.

What are the unseen blessings of sending groups? Although there has been a great deal written in the last few years about the damage short-term missions can do, you would be hard-pressed to find one organization that hosts groups who doesn't want more. Why is this? What's the disconnect? Don't they see or understand the damage groups bring? Of course they see it, but the benefits to the missions organizations and people in the field far outweigh the headaches of hosting most groups. How many orphanages, churches, schools, or medical centers would not exist without the teams that built them or support them? How many long-term missionaries would not be on the field today if they had not first taken a short-term trip? When done correctly, short-term missions is world changing.

"First, do no harm" is one of the tenants of the Hippocratic Oath, which is central to the medical profession. The same idea is critical to a healthy approach to short-term missions. So often we rush in with well-meaning intentions but wind up making the situation worse than it already is.

Often, at first glance, a missions idea to "help" might sound excellent, like an act of generosity. Yet the results of our actions might ripple out in ways we have never considered.

Here at our orphanage, we've had well-meaning people visit and pass out loose change to our kids. They think they're blessing the kids when they see them light up at receiving this money. However, if you were visiting a family in the U.S., would you randomly pass out cash to their kids? It's just weird. Also, by groups doing this, it teaches our kids to beg or manipulate guests in our home. Before they came to us, many of our children were begging to survive. We try *very* hard to teach our kids how to work for extras in life and not to beg. By people kindly passing out quarters, they're working directly against some of our goals here with the children in our care.

I've seen well-meaning groups come into a community, find a local pastor, and offer to build a church building from the ground up. On the surface, it might sound great. In a bigger picture, fully funding a church build usually sets up an unhealthy dynamic. Does that congregation have emotional ownership of their church if they have no skin in the game? Are they learning to share and give to the church if they think their "widow's mite" isn't needed? It's incredibly healthy when a congregation comes together to work toward a common goal. I'm not saying we shouldn't support and help churches in the mission field, but by doing everything for them, we're not allowing them to grow in a normal healthy fashion.

Broadening Perspective; Building Relationship

So what's the solution? How do we go on a mission trip and not do more harm than good? The best way to move forward with any mission trip is to prayerfully consider our impact, both positive and negative, in any community we're going to serve. Just as people are the center of the problem with missions, they're also the heart of the solution. Along with prayer, the single most crucial thing we can do is to develop a relationship with, and listen to, an on-the-ground ministry already serving long-term in that area. These are the people whose ministries are either blessed by your visit—or are left to clean up the rubble. They know what works, what doesn't work, and how to leverage the skills and resources you want to provide. Let them guide you into a productive, helpful trip for all involved.

Here is one example of how subtly shifting a project will bring it from harmful to beneficial: We have teams that want to do food distribution for families in impoverished areas. They often hit up Walmart in a nearby city, buy lots of groceries in bulk, and bag them up for distribution. Yes, they are providing food and a blessing for families in the community. But what are they doing to the local minimarts and farmers markets? Most small stores are barely staying open with what little sales they have in needier areas. The result of this short-term blessing might be people in the community losing jobs. If that same group buys locally, they might pay a little more for the groceries, but along with blessing the families in need, they would also be pouring money into the local community and helping to keep businesses and jobs moving forward.

With subtle, wise shifting, our efforts can have the desired positive impact that we want to bring. Maybe instead of passing out loose change to kids in an orphanage, we can find ways to bless the overworked staff who most people ignore. Whether it's food or construction materials, consider buying locally whenever possible. Perhaps for every person on our team pouring that concrete slab, we commit to hiring a local construction worker to help for the day.

Different Kinds of Trips

"Short-term missions" can fit any number of goals, and it's advantageous to you and your team to set those goals early in the planning stages; then reevaluate the goals as you build relationships on the ground in your destination country or area. Let's look at a few common goals:

14

- *The evangelistic trip.* The purpose and goal of the trip is the spread of the Gospel, or to assist those on the ground doing evangelistic work. These trips might include participating in local church services, performing evangelistic dramas, teaching Bible studies, etc.

- *The construction service trip.* The purpose of the trip is to assist those on the ground through supplies and physical labor. Sometimes it can be as simple as cleaning up and painting or as involved and skill heavy as constructing schools, homes, medical clinics, or other needed physical structures, such as water wells and small farms.

- *The emergency needs trip.* These types of trips are rarer but just as critical: sending skilled teams and supplies to assist after emergency situations, such as earthquakes, flooding, hurricane relief, etc.

- *The high skills trip.* These trips usually involve medical outreach and training but can also include IT support or assistance, small business training, management training, etc.

- *The* voluntourism *trip.* This term has come up in recent years meant to make fun of what many mission trips have become—wrapping a vacation with the mantle of doing good deeds. I personally have no problem with a voluntourism trip, if good work is being done and relationships are being built. My hope is that every team I host enjoys their trip and has a life-changing experience. Travel expands our horizons and broadens us as individuals. If our travel includes meeting, serving, and working with great people from other countries, this is a great thing. The key is to be honest and realistic about our goals.

Becoming a Good Partner

We have set some ambitious goals for the book you're now reading. We want to take a fresh look at short-term missions and guide people into healthy reciprocal mission relationships. Healthy relationships are always reciprocal—they work in both directions as people learn to serve each other and build each other up. We all have something to learn, and we all have something to offer when we bump up against other Christians in whatever part of the world we might be working in.

As we continue, we'll be looking at some core components of missions: motivations for going and hosting, how to have a positive impact and do as little harm as possible, the thorny issue of financing in missions, and several other areas that are critical to look at if you're going to have an effective, healthy, reciprocal short-term mission experience.

No matter the topic we're discussing, our main goal is to flip the normal missions model—"we have something to give, and we need to go save those people over there"—and instead show the value of a truly reciprocal relationship and how to build one. Yes, you and your team have some wonderful talents and resources to offer, but many churches, ministries, and people around the world also have tremendous and valuable gifts to offer to you and your team. We all bring something to the table. When we open our perspectives and our hearts, God can use all of us to inspire each other and bring meaningful change in our lives.

Our hope and prayer is that this book encourages you to start, or improve, your short-term mission experience and efforts. May God direct your thoughts, conversations, and efforts in missions, and every area.

Phil's 2 Cents

You don't know what you don't know until you know it. We all have blind spots. We all have areas of our lives that we cannot see unless someone else reveals them to us, especially in a cross-cultural setting. No matter where we go, we take our context, our culture and how we see the world with us. This is not bad or wrong, but we must be aware that our view or understanding of the place and people we are serving has blind spots. There are things we just don't know. If we want to be effective on our short-term mission trips, we need to be available to be taught and led by those we are serving.

Reciprocal humble relationships are the best way we can grow and have our blind spots revealed to us. Choosing ignorance over discovering a way to do short-term missions that honors, respects and serves everyone is counter to God's command to "love your neighbor." If we want to do short-term missions well and effectively where everyone involved benefits from the short-term mission trip we must be willing to have open and honest relationships with those we are serving. As short-term mission trip teams and leaders, we must be willing to hear from the host communities about the damage we are doing, and be led into how we can change and partner with them to more effectively further the Kingdom of God.

CHAPTER 2

A Biblical Vision for Short-Term Missions

Phil

I live in a place where I see countless short-term mission trip teams. They are easy to pick out with their matching bright shirts—at the airport, at In-N-Out, or at the Costco before crossing the border—and the endless parade of white 15-passenger vans. You know who they are and their mission as you read their theme verse on the back of their shirts.

People have many reasons for going on a short-term mission trip. Some go because they believe it is the next step in their relationship with God to serve "the least of these" and to "preach the Gospel to the ends of the earth." Yet others go because they don't know what else to do with their summer vacation, so why not go and make a difference on a short-term mission trip.

There are many good reasons for going. But some seemingly good reasons, if we are not mindful, aren't always helpful. Though the Bible does not explicitly talk about short-term missions, it gives us the framework for effective short-term missions. In this chapter, we'll look at what the Bible says about the purpose of short-term missions and how we've seen those purposes play out in real life.

The World Is Broken

It doesn't take much to realize that our world is broken. Marriages are falling apart. In the U.S. alone, the number of children in foster care continues to increase, homelessness is on the rise, and mass shootings continue to claim more lives. Globally there are over 28 million people still in slavery today and approximately 153 million orphans. Our brokenness can be seen in how we treat each other and care for God's creation. We have all felt it. No one is exempt.

All the hurt and pain can be traced back to the broken relationships we have with God, ourselves, each other, and this world. What's weird is that no one taught us to disobey or hurt each other—it is part of our human nature.

I remember the first time my son deliberately disobeyed me. He couldn't have been more than 12 months old. He was sitting on our kitchen floor playing when he opened a cupboard door under the sink and started touching the cleaning supplies that were stored there. Sure, maybe we should have had child safety locks, but this kid usually didn't need them. I said, "Caleb ... NO!" I chose not to shut the cabinet because I wanted to see if he would obey me. He looked at me and went back to touching the items under the sink. This time I grabbed his hand, looked him in his eyes with a serious expression, and with more intensity in my voice, I said, "Caleb ... NO! Don't touch that." He looked at me and with disgust in his eyes, grunted at me, and touched the cleaning supplies again. I was in shock! This was my compliant firstborn. How could this cute, chubby-faced toddler disobey me like that? Even more so, who taught him to disobey me?

Simple stories like this happen in every relationship in our lives. Why do we live in a world where relationships are broken? Where did our relationships with each other go wrong?

The Beginning of Brokenness

Our brokenness is nothing new. In Genesis 3 we read about when our world was broken for the first time:

"Did God really say, 'You must not eat from any tree in the garden'?" The woman said to the serpent, "We may eat fruit from the trees in the garden, but God did say, 'You must not eat fruit from the tree that is in the middle of the garden, and you must not touch it, or you will die.'" The serpent said, "You will not certainly die, for God knows that when you eat from it your eyes will be opened, and you will be like God, knowing good and evil."

When the woman saw that the fruit of the tree was good for food and pleasing to the eye, and also desirable for gaining wisdom, she took some and ate it. She also gave some to her husband, who was with her, and he ate it. Then the eyes of both of them were opened.

When Adam and Eve heard the sound of God walking in the garden, they hid. But God called to them, "Where are you?"

"Where are you?" I have often wondered why God asked this question. Of course He knows where Adam and Eve are hiding: He is all knowing and all present.

I believe the question has to do more with drawing their attention to the location of Adam and Eve's heart and their relationship with God, than it did with their physical location.[1] "Where are you?" emotionally? spiritually? mentally? and relationally? It's like when you have a conversation with someone and they seem to be somewhere else mentally or emotionally. You can tell something's changed. Something had changed in the relationship between Adam, Eve, and God. So I sense God was asking, "What happened to our relationship?"

The serpent was half right; isn't that how Satan works many times? When he said, "You will not certainly die" (3:4), Adam and Eve did not physically die at that moment, but their relationship as they knew it with God, themselves, each other, and creation all experienced death.

---

[1] I first heard this interpretation of this text in a sermon from Matt Krick, BayMarin Community Church

- Adam and Eve's relationship as they knew it died. They would never again experience sinless intimacy. They began blaming someone else for their disobedience (3:12-13; 16).

- Adam and Eve's relationship with God as they knew it died. They were kicked out of the garden, never to walk in the "cool of the day" with Him again on earth (3:23).

- Adam and Eve's relationship with the earth died, as now they would need to work the soil, being dependent upon the weather and battling weeds and thorns to grow crops (3:17-19).

Their broken relationships were passed down to their family when, just a chapter later in Genesis, we read of jealousy, selfishness, pride, and murder between Adam and Eve's two sons, Cain and Abel (4:1-12). Then in Genesis 6 God flooded the earth because of the sin and broken relationships that had invaded the world. The brokenness has been passed down from generation to generation ever since. Death has come into our relationships. From our individual choices to slavery, poverty, unjust laws, and war—all our relationships are broken.

What does this have to do with short-term missions? Well, would we go on short-term mission trips if our world wasn't broken? Most short-term mission trips go to places where our world is visibly broken with a desire to bring hope and healing to the brokenness. To think more deeply about this, we need to think about God's intentions for evil in the world and what the Genesis story shows about God's plan.

Does God Intend Evil?

The story of God and the Garden of Eden raises questions about God and evil. The role of evil is something that I have always wrestled with. Almost every trip someone asks, "Why is there so much suffering in the world?" Yes, suffering can cause us to draw closer to Him, and God doesn't waste anything. Great theologians have wrestled with the role of evil, and regardless of where we fall in our beliefs, when you look at the back of a boy that has been beaten by a slave master or see 10,000-12,000 children abandoned on the streets in Tijuana, we can't ignore the tension that exists.

When we witness pain and suffering on our short-term mission trips, it makes us feel uncomfortable. Sometimes in an attempt to feel better, we too quickly try to resolve very complex issues. For those who lead short-term missions, as well as those who host short-term missions, let's think critically about these deeper issues and wrestle with the tensions they create.

The questions I have considered as they relate to short-term mission trips are: If, as many believe, suffering is part of God's plan, why should we even go on short-term mission trips? If there is a reason for poverty, slavery, starvation, and people not having access to clean water, then why are we getting in the way of God's plan by going on these trips? Should we be working to alleviate pain and suffering around the world?

The story in Genesis is a portrait of God's desire for perfect relationship with humankind. Through disobedience our world broke, ushering in pain and suffering. Jesus came to redeem it all. The amazing thing about God is that He is capable of making something good come from the ashes. Jesus reveals to us His desire to bring hope and healing into people's lives through relationships, and if we desire to be like Him, we can join Him not only on our trips, but in our everyday lives as well.

How Jesus Responds to Suffering

Jesus reveals to us how He feels about the brokenness and pain in our world in the story of raising His friend Lazarus from the dead (John 11). Lazarus had been sick and was near death. Mary and Martha, Lazarus' sisters, had sent word to Jesus that Lazarus was very sick and asked Jesus to come quickly. Yet, when Jesus heard that Lazarus was sick, He stayed two extra days before departing for Lazarus' house.

When Jesus arrived in the town, Lazarus had already been in the grave for 4 days (John 11:17). As Jesus approached the house, Mary and Martha ran to see Him. They were distraught at the death of their brother and friend. They were also upset that Jesus had not come sooner, as they believed that Lazarus would not have died had Jesus arrived earlier.

When Jesus is met with human suffering, seeing the pain on His friends' faces, Jesus responds in a surprising way. "When Jesus saw her weeping, and the Jews who had come along with her also weeping, he was *deeply moved in spirit and troubled*" (John 11:33, emphasis mine).

The Greek word for: "deeply moved in spirit" is *embrimaomai*, which means "to be moved with anger." If Jesus was moved with anger, why was He angry? Or a better question: who or what was He angry at? Was Jesus angry with the lack of faith on the part of Mary, Martha, and the people around Him? Was Jesus angry at the Jews around Him who would soon want to stone Him? Was Jesus angry that His friend Lazarus died, even though He knew that Lazarus would die?

Perhaps it isn't any of those reasons. Could it be possible that Jesus was angry that there was so much pain and suffering in the world? He was angry that death was part of life. The world as it is was never what God intended.

Following Christ's example of responding to suffering, short-term missions should be focused on alleviating the brokenness in our world. It is good and right for us to walk alongside our friends and family who are suffering, partner with organizations that are doing the daily, hard work of justice, mercy, and compassion in different areas of the world (locally and globally). It is good and right for those who are on the front lines of ministry to work against injustices and poverty, care for orphans, and provide food and clean water.

Working with partner organizations, short-term missions have helped release the weights and shackles from people's lives so that they can grow more fully into the people God has created them to become, through orphanages and schools, medical clinics, sustainable housing, clean water, or churches built to reach those who are far from Jesus.

But because short-term missions work so closely with the hurt in the world, and since they're capable of bringing God's purposes, there is potential for doing harm even when we intend to alleviate it. We must be cautious in how we facilitate our short-term mission trips. We need to understand that we are not the Messiah, and we cannot and should not lead these short-term mission trips alone. Since the very root of the problem in the world is broken relationships, our relationships are a key to bringing God's hope and healing. To do this, we need to develop long-term relationships with those we are serving on our trips, and we need to acknowledge that brokenness exists on both sides of the relationship.

We All Need to Be Rescued

One of the many things I've learned over the course of leading short-term mission trips is that it's not only those who are living in poverty and on the streets who need to be rescued. I need rescuing. I need to be saved from my individualistic, consumeristic, me-first life. The students and adults I lead on our trips are in need of saving too—saving from apathy, addiction, depression, broken relationships, emptiness, loneliness—and in need of the loving arms of Jesus. Our poverty is not as easily seen as physical poverty, street children, or tarp houses. We are able to hide it behind manicured lawns, busyness, the veil of independence, and wealth, appearing to have it all together.

Though we live in different places surrounded by vastly different circumstances, we need the people we are serving on our short-term mission trips just as much, if not more, than they need us. We can learn a lot from those we serve, understanding that we have a mutual need of being "saved." God has hidden the remedy of our brokenness in unlikely places. The people we are serving are rich in perspective and wisdom that can help us remove the weights and shackles that are keeping us from becoming the people God has created us to be.

Let's talk about poverty for a minute. I'm sure you have heard the stats that if you were to turn the population of the world into a Village of 100 people,[2] proportionately you would get the following results:

- 6 people would own 59% of the entire village's wealth, and all 6 would be from the U.S.

- 74 people would own 39% of the entire village's wealth

- 20 people would share the remaining 2% of the entire village's wealth

- 80 would live in substandard housing

- 12 would be unable to read

- 50 would be malnourished, 20 don't have a reliable source of food, 30 always have enough to eat

- 1 would have a college degree

- 80 would have clean water and 20 would not

[2] "If The World Were a Village of 100," University of Southern Maine, accessed, November, 2017. https://usm.maine.edu/international/if-world-were-village-100-0

- If you keep your food in a refrigerator and your clothes in a closet, if you have a bed to sleep in and a roof over your head, you are richer than 75% of the entire world population.

These are staggering facts about the disparity between privilege and need. Where do you find yourself in these statistics? Chances are you are at least in the top 10%-20%. With much privilege comes the opportunity and responsibility to make a difference. But the price of privilege comes at a high cost. Poverty isn't always physical and materialistic.

- The United States consumes more opioids than another country in the world, and it is growing.[3]

- The United States has more people die of overdosing on drugs than any other country in the world.[4]

- According to the World Health Organization, the United States tops the list of citizens who experiencing bipolar disorder, major depressive disorder, or chronic minor depression over the course of a year.

- The World Economic Forum published the "World's Happiest Countries" and the United States ranked 13th. But what was interesting is that the most affluent coun-

---

[3] Keith Humphreys, "Americans use far more opioids than anyone else in the world" March 20, 2017.
https://www.washingtonpost.com/news/wonk/wp/2017/03/15/american s-use-far-more-opioids-than-anyone-else-in-the-world/?noredirect=on&utm_term=.aaa75453fb25

[4] Dyfed Loesche, "America Has the Highest Drug-Death Rate in North America-and the World," Statista. June 26, 2017.
https://www.statista.com/chart/9973/drug-related-deaths-and-mortality-rate-worldwide/

tries ranked near the bottom of the world's happiest index. Money does not equate to happiness.[5]

- According to the UN's Demographics and Social Statistics Division, the United States ranks 10th out of 196 in the world in divorce rates.

- Studies have shown that happiness or contentment with life does not improve once a person is making $75,000/year.[6]

- The United States is the largest consumer of products in the world.[7]

What gives? The United States is one of the wealthiest countries in the world with the most opportunity to have whatever we want, yet we suffer the most anxiety, depression, and unhappiness compared to many other countries. We are suffering a type of poverty that is easy to hide.

Thomas Merton put it best when he wrote, "People may spend their whole lives climbing the ladder of success only to find, once they reach the top, that the ladder is leaning against the wrong wall." Are we as Americans climbing the ladder of success on the wrong wall?

In Luke 19 Jesus visited Zacchaeus, the wealthy chief tax collector. Zacchaeus, who was a Jew, collected taxes for Rome. Therefore he was hated by the Jewish people because he worked for the oppressive Roman government. Zacchaeus was not only hated because people viewed him as a traitor, but because he obtained his wealth

---

[5] Keith Breene, "The world's happiest countries in 2016" November 14, 2016. https://www.weforum.org/agenda/2016/11/the-worlds-happiest-countries-in-2016/
[6] Susie Poppick "The Money Happiness Connection" June 10, 2014. http://time.com/money/2802147/does-money-buy-happiness/
[7] The 25 Largest Consumer's Markets ... And The Outlook For 2015" International Business Guide. accessed November 2017. https://www.internationalbusinessguide.org/25-largest-consumers-markets-outlook-2015/

by cheating and extorting people out of their money. Zacchaeus was destroying people's lives. He was not living in a right relationship with God, himself, or others. Zacchaeus, like many people, was pursuing power and wealth. This pursuit had turned into weights and shackles keeping him from becoming all that God had created him to be. Our own pursuits of power, wealth, and status are weights that will keep us from becoming all that God has created us to be. Yet Jesus pursued Zacchaeus.

Jesus, Zacchaeus, and other "sinners" had dinner together. After they had finished their meal, Zacchaeus stood up and made a startling announcement. "Look, Lord! Here and now I give half of my possessions to the poor, and if I have cheated anybody out of anything, I will pay back four times the amount" (19:8). Zacchaeus, in a moment, realized that his pursuit of power and wealth was destroying not only his life, but other people's lives. Jesus then said to Zacchaeus, "Today salvation has come to this house" (19:9). Zaccheaus realized that the best way to live was to give his life away, reconcile relationships with those he had destroyed, and begin living in right relationships with God, himself and others.

There are physical and material weights keeping people in the majority world (countries not considered first world countries) and parts of the United States from becoming the people God has created them to be—weights such as poverty, lack of food and clean water, slavery, oppression, and other injustices. Yet many Americans are suffering a different kind of poverty that is keeping us from realizing spiritual, relational, and mental wholeness. Through relationships with those we are serving, we can help remove the weights and shackles off of each other's lives and hearts. This is what it means to have a reciprocal relationship. We need each other to help alleviate the poverty in our own lives.

Short-term missions can be done in a way where we minister to each other. Not from a consumeristic, savior complex way, but from a reciprocal, humble servant way that constantly thinks of others before ourselves and honors everyone's dignity.

If we are honest with ourselves, many of us go on short-term mission trips because we are looking for something. We go seeking to discover what we are missing or what is holding us back. In fact, we go looking for salvation. We are looking for something more to this life. We believe that this can't be all there is. We are looking to live into a bigger story than the one we are currently living. So we go because, deep down, we know we need it. The truth is we might need those we are going to serve more than they need us. When we step into a reciprocal relationship, we will experience the salvation that we can offer each other.

A Vision for Reciprocal Missions

One of the often overlooked passages in Scripture is John 13:34-35. Jesus was with His disciples in the upper room before He was betrayed by Judas and handed over to the Pharisees. During their discussion, and right after Jesus predicted Peter's betrayal, Jesus said, "A new command I give you: Love one another." At first glance, this is not a new command. We have heard this before.

In Matthew one of the "experts in the law" tested Jesus by asking Him what is the greatest commandment in the Law. Jesus responded, "'Love the Lord your God with all your heart and with all your soul and with all your mind.' This is the first and greatest commandment. And the second is like it: 'Love your neighbor as yourself'" (Matthew 22:37-39).

I'm sure we have all heard these verses in Matthew and John. But if we were to dig a little deeper, we will discover that what Jesus was commanding His disciples to do in the upper room takes it up another level.

First Jesus said that we should "love one another." "One another" in the Greek is one word, *allelous*—it is a reciprocal pronoun. A reciprocal pronoun is used when two or more people are carrying out or have carried out a similar action with both receiving mutual benefit or consequence.

Here is how I have experienced this in my life: A few years ago I attended a cross country meet of two of the students from my youth group. I found a place where there weren't any other spectators so they could hear me as they ran by: "Nice job! Keep going! You are doing great! Relax your arms! Catch the person in front of you!" Later that spring, the same students hosted a 5K road race to raise funds and bring awareness to modern-day slavery in the cosmetic industry. I signed up to run, and though I've always been a competitive runner, I hadn't trained in more than 5 months. I wanted to quit. As I was rounding the curve where I planned to give up and walk, there were the two girls that I had cheered on during their cross country race: "Don't stop now! Keep going! You can do it! You are almost there! Catch the person in front of you!" With their encouragement, I finished.

By encouraging each other during our races, we all enjoy the benefits and joy of finishing. We showed love to "one another." We received mutual benefit for our act of care and love for each other during the race.

When we step into our short-term mission trips, we should look at these experiences as a reciprocal relationship. Our relationship should be mutually benefiting, and it is up to us, the trip goers, to do the hard work of being sure we are helping to facilitate a reciprocal relationship.

It's interesting that Paul, the great missionary of the New Testament, mentioned the importance of a reciprocal relationship when he wrote to the Romans: "I long to see you so that I may impart to you some spiritual gift to make you strong—that is, that you and I may be *mutually encouraged by each other's faith*" (Romans 1:11-12, emphasis mine). This is what we should hope and long for on our short-term mission trips—that we can encourage each other in our faith, our journey toward Jesus, removing each other's weights, loosening each other's shackles, becoming all that God has created us to become.

But in John 13:34-35, Jesus didn't stop with just "love one another." He told us *how* we should love one another. "A new command I give you: Love one another as *I have loved you*" (emphasis mine).

The love that Jesus showed, not only to His disciples but to the world, was a sacrificial, others-first love that went beyond how I love myself. As we know, Jesus went to the cross for us. He laid down His life so that we might have life.

Sacrificing on a short-term mission trip may look different than just sacrificing a week of vacation or time away from family. Sacrificing on a short-term mission trip may look like giving up your agenda for the agenda of the host community. Sacrifice may look like not forcing your way of doing ministry on the local church. Sacrifice may look like submitting your leadership to the leadership of the ministry you are serving with on your trip. Sacrifice may look like not doing the VBS you had planned on doing. Sacrifice on a short-term mission trip looks like yielding your needs, wants, and agenda to the needs, wants, and agenda of the host community.

Not only is the short-term mission trip team sacrificing, but so are our hosts. When our short-term mission teams come on these trips to work with orphanages, medical clinics, churches, and other ministries, we need to understand that we triple their workload. The amazing thing is, these ministry hosts are willing to do the extra work for us to come without complaining! Not only are they now serving us, meeting our basic needs of food, shelter, setting up work projects for us, and meeting our other needs, but they are still running their ministries at the same time. They don't stop what they are doing while providing for our needs. Their hospitality is amazing! We may not realize it, but they have been preparing to host us for almost as long as we have been preparing to come.

In Philippians 2 Paul urged us to have the same attitude and mindset as Christ. Let us live and act this way as we journey onto our short-term mission trips, build reciprocal relationships, and live sacrificially for one another.

Reciprocal Missions

Embracing Each Other

As we serve together, mission trip goer and mission trip host, there is no *us* and *them*. There is just *us*. We are both suffering the effects of the pain and brokenness of this world. We are both in need of saving. We are both in need of what each other has to offer in helping reconcile ourselves to God, each other, and this world. If we who go on short-term mission trips step down from the pedestal and position ourselves as learners and servants, and if those who host groups position themselves as not those who are just receivers but are ministers of the Gospel to those who come, we will be able to remove the weights and shackles off each other's lives so that we can become who God has created us to be. Through reciprocal relationships we can join God in bringing hope and healing to our broken world.

DJ's 2 Cents

We all have something to share; we all have something to give. It is important that we go out and interact with others and share with each other. This sounds basic, but it's easy to get comfortable in our own circle, in our own church, and not to seek outside interaction.

Biblically, it's clear that we are one body. We might have different parts, but we are all vital and all have something to bring to the party. I always found it interesting that when Jesus shared the "Our Father" prayer with His apostles, it was a corporate prayer. There is not a single personal pronoun in the prayer, but the words "us," "we," and "our" are used over and over again. It's obvious from the Gospels that we are one family and need to interact as such.

As one who hosts a great deal of teams while running a large ministry in Mexico, I can fully appreciate the need for healthy reciprocal relationships. When short-term missions are done right, everybody wins, everybody shares, and everyone leaves blessed through the experience. Through living out the example of biblical community, our lives are changed for the better.

Yes, the teams bring resources and labor, but they also come with their own hurts, needs, and a desire for more of God, whether they realize it or not. As hosts, we have so much to offer the visiting teams in the way of education, guidance, and helping them experience God in ways they've only dreamt of.

CHAPTER 3

Troubleshooting Short-Term Missions

Phil

A few years ago I participated in a weekend learning retreat with other youth pastors, ministry leaders, and church volunteers. We were exploring issues along the border between Mexico and the United States. The first night of the retreat we were sitting around a conference table, and the facilitator asked us to introduce ourselves and what we do at our respective churches and ministries. The first person introduced themselves as someone who had been delegated to lead their church's short-term mission trip to Mexico. She lamented that she did not like short-term mission trips and that it was her goal to "kill the sacred cow." The next person jumped on the bandwagon of bashing short-term missions and stated that it was his goal to end short-term missions at his church as well. The conversation continued to snowball as people gave reason after reason why short-term missions wasn't working.

Then it was my turn. I sat there nervous, not knowing exactly what to say or how to say it. I thought about taking the easy way out and saying that I was an Outreach Pastor at a church in California or that I was in the process of getting my master's degree in social justice. Both were true, but that's not the entire story. What do you say when everyone in the room is bashing the very thing you are passionate about?

Inside I agreed with just about everything they were saying and about why short-term missions should end. Their words had truth and merit. But I also knew that the American church approach to short-term missions is antiquated and ineffective and sometimes dangerously harmful. Yet I know the solution isn't to throw the baby out with the bathwater.

"Hi, my name is Phil Steiner, and I am the director of an organization called Be2Live. We lead short-term service and learning trips to Mexico and Ghana."

An awkward silence fell over the room as nobody knew what to say. Nobody moved. People diverted eye contact from me.

I continued, "We are working on reenvisioning short-term mission trips so that they are meaningful and mutually beneficial. I believe that there is a way to do short-term missions well, and we need to find a new way forward."

While many call for doing away with short-term mission trips, they likely aren't going away, nor do I think they should. But what the others at the retreat said is true—many mistakes have harmed ministries, cultures, and people, so we must be wise in how we approach our short-term mission trips. Our vision, motivation, and execution must be well thought out. Before moving forward in doing short-term missions well, we need to be honest about the damage that has been done to communities in which we have served. We don't want to perpetuate the damage of the past, especially in the name of Jesus.

Historically the damage done on short-term mission trips has been because we haven't taken the time to think about or understand what we are doing and the ramifications of our focus and actions.

Reciprocal Missions

We don't know what we don't know. If we understood what was happening below the surface, we would change how we lead short-term missions. Because of our ignorance, we continue to make the same mistakes over and over again. When we work in a cross-cultural setting, we must be aware of the different nuances that are taking place below the surface, and ask for help when the nuances are beyond our understanding. If it is not your first culture, this will take a lot of time, asking questions and listening.

We had been sending a few teams annually to Mexico for six years when we started working at a new orphanage. The first time we met with the director, he said to do whatever God laid on our heart to do. We had been around long enough to know that this is a dangerous answer. We also knew that culturally Mexicans are not as direct as Americans. The more we hung out at the orphanage, the more we saw the results of people doing what they felt "God led them to do" without helpful direction. There was a skateboard ramp that warped quickly and became a safety hazard in a community where there is limited access to medical care. The most glaring was a big beautiful stage in the center of the property. The exposed wood was not yet painted and a roof protected it from the elements, yet the orphanage had not used it once in the two years since it had been built by a well-meaning American group that did whatever they felt God led them to do. Ironically, on the other side of the orphanage sat a shell of a boys dorm that had been in need of finishing for the past five years. The money and wood spent on the stage would have gone a long way in completing the boys dorm. If the leaders of the mission group had taken the time to sit, listen, and understand the needs of the orphanage beyond the director's first response, their resources could have been put to good use.

The following are arguments against short-term missions and suggestions for creating a new pathway forward.

Problem: Short-Term Mission Teams Take Local Jobs

Short-term mission teams should not do a job that local workers would do. Yes, I agree with this statement. When we bring our team to build a house, orphanage, medical center, or church, it is likely that the team is taking jobs away from able-bodied locals. Let that sink in a little. Even though it may be painting a wall, pouring concrete, or building a house, chances are there are locals in the community who would love to get paid the minimum wage for that job. Why not build into your project funds to hire local tradespeople to work alongside your group?

But here is the interesting twist. The largest consumer in the United States is the American teenager. The money spent on restaurants, grocery stores, lodging, construction supplies, and souvenirs by young short-term mission teams in local communities is astronomical. Short-term missions should and do boost the overall economy of the communities we serve. In planning trips, be intentional about how you can buy your supplies, food, and invest in the overall health of the local economy.

The bigger issue with this argument is based on financial logic. Nearly all nonprofits and ministries that are working to meet the real tangible needs of people are working on a shoestring budget. If a ministry could afford to hire local workers to do their construction projects, they would gladly do it. But many don't have the financial means to pay for the project supplies and the labor. They don't have the resources to further their vision in reaching their community, so they depend on short-term mission teams to help provide the needed resources.

Many people then reply, "Well, just send money and don't go on the trip." Yes, it is true that most ministries would much rather you just send money to help their organization. But in the long run, experiencing the ministry leads to more long-term financial commitments. If people can touch, feel, and see what the ministry is doing to reach people by going on the trip and joining in the vision, they can make a connection that leads to monthly support or future fundraising projects.

We recently led a church on a spring break trip to Mexico. They worked at one of our partner sites, a medical clinic that was being built to meet the physical, emotional, and spiritual needs of the local community. This community did not have access to any affordable health care for even basic needs, and although the clinic had been operating out of two small rooms in the local church, they had outgrown their space. Four years ago they were able to purchase land and began building a medical clinic, predominantly through short-term mission teams.

The pastor of this church was touched by their vision and, knowing the clinic was significantly far from its financial goal, went home and shared news of the ministry with a local foundation. After much prayer and discussion, the foundation decided to fund the rest of the project. Almost immediately the medical clinic hired more local labor to help complete the clinic.

Relationships can develop that are bigger than your one week. Leverage your networks by connecting people's hearts and passions to the vision and mission of the ministries you are serving. It's all for the Kingdom. Americans can see inspiring possibilities of hope, and ministries can get the support they need to bring change to local communities. This is not limited to big givers. Many of the students and adults we have taken on our short-term mission trip are now monthly supporting children in the communities they served. Without the trip, they would not be sending money on a monthly basis to support these ministries or advocating for them back home. A reciprocal relationship has long-term benefits for everyone involved.

Problem: Short-Term Mission Teams Demotivate the Local Community

Some communities receive hundreds of American short-term mission participants every year. These short-term mission teams build houses and provide clothing, food, and other supplies. Due to the pure volume of visiting teams, this can create an unhealthy dependency of people in the community on short-term mission teams.

There becomes a sentiment among the community: "The Americans will take care of it." There can be an expectation that the Americans will solve their problems and meet their needs. As a result of this dependency, apathy, laziness, and even anger can become an issue for the people who live in the host community.

We recently had dinner with a Mexican family who lives in a community that receives a lot of short-term mission groups. This couple works at a local school and daycare in the community. They described how they wanted to motivate the students in their community to work and to serve others, but it's been a struggle.

I asked them, "Do you think that with all the youth groups and short-term mission teams that come into the community to serve and work, they have the mentality that the Americans will do the work, and it creates laziness in the Mexican students?"

Without hesitation they said, "Yes."

If we are aware of this possibility for unhealthy dependence, we can better approach how to facilitate less harm to the community. Once again this is where a long-term investment in relationship is so important. When you partner with local organizations that understand the nuances of the community, the relationship can better address dependency. A reciprocal relationship is not afraid of hard conversations like this because we want the best for everyone involved, including those not directly affected by a group's presence in the community. A relationship like this takes time but builds trust and allows for vulnerable conversations about the effect a group has on the community, positively and negatively, and the flexibility to change the approach so that everyone benefits.

What good is it if we do good for one week but nothing changes when we leave? When we at Be2Live facilitate our trips, if there are not already local workers on our project then we plan for a portion of our project cost to pay for local workers to work alongside us. One of our values is we want to do projects *with* people and not *for* them. When we do projects for people, we can dehumanize them and make them feel like they are the project. But when we partner with them and work together, we give honor and dignity, and our relationships and understanding grow.

Here's an example of the damage that comes from doing a project *for* someone. A short-term mission team wanted to build a house for a family. The family was selected by an organization that had a relationship with the family. When the team arrived to work on this family's new house, the father and son of the family showed up the same time ready to go to work with the American team. With good intentions, the leader of the team told the father and son to "rest" and just let them do the work. The first day the father and son sat by and occasionally picked up a shovel to help move the sand into buckets for the concrete. But the father and son were quickly told just to let the group do the work. Eventually the father and son left and never came back. When it came time for the house dedication, the family was there, but the father and son stood in the back and quietly took the keys to the house that the group built. The short-term mission team was excited to have built this house for the family, but the father and son felt embarrassed over the whole situation because they were not invited into the project to provide for their family.

The difference between *for* and *with* isn't something I've always understood. Three years ago we wanted to support one of our partner organizations at Christmas time. They asked us to provide Christmas gifts for their volunteers who work with families living in the old Tijuana dump. The volunteers of the ministry also live on the dump. We were told to bring gift bags for each family member. We got names, gender, and clothing sizes of each person. We put the word out to our church, and the giving was overwhelming. The day of the Christmas party came. We set the gifts under the tree. Everyone was excited about the food and the community. There was a buzz in the air. It was fun seeing people we had worked with on our trips. The director asked us to pass out the gifts to the volunteers and their families. As our staff passed out the gifts, we felt a sudden awkwardness. Our heart was to celebrate and support these people who had welcomed us into their community and served sacrificially every day. But this one act felt like the "haves" giving to the "have nots." and it made us sad to be the ones passing out gifts to children while their parents looked on, knowing it was something they could never provide. We left that party realizing we had to do it differently next year.

The next year we were more intentional to celebrate in a way that strengthened the community and the individual families. We still collected gifts for children and adults from our church and community in the United States—new clothes, shoes, tools, makeup, and other needed and fun items. The day of the party we set up a Christmas store for the parents to select gifts for their children and the children to choose for their parents. The anticipation of shopping for their family was contagious, as was the care in which the children took to pick the perfect gift for their parents. Volunteers wrapped the gifts, and the families took the gifts home for their own celebration. Sure, it is fun to get caught up in the party spirit, and no there weren't any photos of cute little kids opening shiny new toys to take back as a thank you report to the churches that donated, but this wasn't about us. The fact that these individuals were honored for their work and their families got to share a special Christmas day in the quietness of their little home was a win in our book. The director of the ministry said the feedback was meaningful. This *with* approach showed the volunteers that we valued their contribution and valued their right to choose for their families. Everyone felt loved and honored because we did Christmas with each other.

Every trip can be transformed by working *with* locals instead of *for* them. When you are on a work site, ask the local organization you are working with to use some of your project money to pay for local workers to join you. If you are working with a family, such as building a house or providing Christmas gifts, always invite the family to join you. This is particularly powerful for fathers and sons, who feel the responsibility to provide for their families. By doing something *for* a family, you take a father's joy in providing and cause him shame about his inability to help. But when he's part of the process, he's empowered to provide for his family and receives the joy that comes with it. Partnering in this way also gives the visiting teams a chance to get to know local people and to be enriched by their perspectives and life stories.

The local people we meet on our short-term mission trips have stories about God that will blow our minds. They have insight and understanding about faith and life that will give us new eyes to see Jesus, God, and Scripture. Many have risked more than we probably ever will and have experienced God in ways we can only imagine. These individuals and their stories will be what our group remembers long after the trip is over.

I have learned a lot from a short, Mexican woman who lives in the old Tijuana dump. Listening to her story, the hardships she has overcome, and watching how she serves and loves her community, I have witnessed her faith in Jesus and her trust in Him daily. She has challenged my walk, as well as helped me understand Jesus in a different way. Through living out her faith, this woman has taught me how to trust Jesus more fully.

A leader of a ministry we work with gave up his comfortable life of retirement to live with some of the poorest of the poor. His example has taught me what it means to "find your life" (Matthew 10:39).

A Mexican man who has every reason to be angry and bitter toward God because of his childhood as an orphan and street kid challenges me with how to love Jesus and others in tangible ways. He and his family have opened their home to foster other orphans. I have witnessed how he loves the men who work for him, always having time to listen and caring more about them as individuals than workers. He has taught me how to sacrificially love others.

The people we meet in another country can help us remember what really matters and teach us new truths about how we can live and act in our part of the world—and we desperately need to listen to them and follow their example in order to be the church God has called us to become. When we find these voices, we should cherish them as long-term friends on a lifelong journey.

Problem: Short-Term Mission Trips Are All About the Visiting Team

For many churches and ministries conducting short-term trips, the focus is primarily, and sometimes only, on the mission team. The participants have paid money to go on a trip, and these are the families who give money to the church so that you can have a dynamic program. Like most situations involving money, the focus is on the consumer. There are expectations of the trip leader about how the mission trip should impact the participants' lives. As a result, our focus can become so much on our group that we end up making demands, shrouded in requests, of the host community or organization, with little regard to the impact it has on the host community or indigenous church.

A large organization wanted to partner with a local ministry on their short-term mission trip by doing some grunt labor to help the ministry save on construction costs. They also wanted relational time with the people in the community, and since their team was made up mostly of high school students they wanted that time to be a soccer camp. Both of these in and of themselves can be great ideas. But the ministry's focus has little to do with children and nothing to do with soccer. Asking an organization that is in the process of constructing a needed building while still meeting real physical needs of the people in the community to put on another program that is outside their scope of ministry is asking a lot.

Initially the leaders of the local ministry said, "No, we don't have the time or resources." But with continued pressure and not wanting to jeopardize the relationship, the local ministry relented and spent extra hours prepping for and sending staff to facilitate and translate for the group so that they could meet their "need" of relational time on their mission trip.

Most short-term mission teams desire relational time with people they're serving. As you can tell, we are big proponents of relationships. To do this well, find an organization or ministry that is already doing work within the community. As you are setting up your trip, express your desire to have good relational time with the people in the community, but don't demand it or dictate how these relationships will be formed or developed. Allow the hosting ministry or organization to provide ways for you to interact that is beneficial for them as well. Even on a project-focused trip, it simply takes being aware: Who is working with you? Who are the people around you that you can start a conversation with while you work or while you are having a meal?

There are countless stories of churches and other ministry organizations that put unneeded pressure on local communities, organizations, and churches to provide particular needs for their participants that is outside the scope of the host organization's work. This type of request does a lot of damage, and it has a ripple effect in the community and into other ministries. We need to understand that when our short-term mission team visits a local ministry, we are adding to their workload. They don't stop their ministry to the community to take care of us; they humbly add us to an already overwhelming workload.

In this self-centered approach, we are using the poor for the benefit of our congregants and participants. Let me say that again. If our primary and only concern is what our mission team is going to get out of the trip, then we are using the poor for our benefit. This approach is not only misguided but is sinful. God is pretty clear about how we should treat the poor.

"One who oppresses the poor to increase his wealth and one who gives gifts to the rich—both come to poverty" (Proverbs 22:16).

"Do not exploit the poor because they are poor and do not crush the needy in court, for the LORD will take up their case and will exact life for life" (Proverbs 22:22-23).

In reciprocal relationships, visiting groups are aware of what our demands and requests do to a local community and the ministries we are working with on our trips. In a reciprocal relationship, there is an open and honest dialogue where hosts can feel the freedom to say, "No," knowing that their refusal will be honored and respected.

While at the same time, the host may help you accomplish your goal, but in a different way. Both sides are learners, leaders, receivers, and givers. We all honor each other so that we can grow and thrive together.

Problem: Short-Term Missions Has Little Long-Term Impact on Those Who Go

Another argument against short-term missions is that it has little to no impact on those who go on the trips. The argument states that within one to three months after participants come back from a short-term mission trip, there is little to no evidence of life change. The mission trip "high" fades, and people forget what they committed to change in their lives and go back to the life they were living before the trip. There is truth to this argument. It is hard to maintain everything you learned and the commitment to live differently when you reenter life back at home. The tsunami of a consumeristic, me-first, competitive culture is difficult to stand against. But is this a good reason *not* to go on a short-term mission trip? I'm sure you would guess my answer is NO!

Though some studies show that short-term mission trips do little to influence many people's lives back at home, there are many who are forever changed. I have not met one long-term missionary who did not first go on a short-term mission trip and hear God's calling on their life. Students who have gone on our trips have started service clubs at their schools, began serving at an elderly home, and got more involved with serving their community. Others have changed their career and school path because of their experience on a short-term mission trip: One student has decided to become a psychologist to work with girls who are enslaved in the sex trafficking industry. Another is majoring in international relationships because she wants to get involved in the refugee crisis. Others are working to become doctors and nurses so they can serve in the majority countries to meet the physical needs of people.

Reciprocal Missions

These students went on a short-term mission trip to offer their service and support to ministries in other countries, and they received inspiration, encouragement, and a perspective on life that they would not have received anywhere else. Many went to the same location multiple times on trips. There is something to be said about investing in the same location a number of times over a number of years that creates lasting impact.

Much of the difference between the results of the studies about the impact of short-term missions and the real-life results I've seen come down to trip leadership, facilitating and processing the mission trip, and relationships built within the community served. Those factors can help overcome the inevitable stress of life that makes change so difficult to sustain, especially for teens.

With the right focus and honed skills, trip leaders can help short-term trips have long-term impact. When we spend too much time focusing on the project we want to accomplish, be it a building, a VBS, or evangelism, we too easily see people and the ministries we are working with as projects or problems to solve instead of people to build relationships with, listen to, and learn from. When we prioritize the relationship with those we are serving over our projects or events, long-term impact happens. Stories are powerful. Relationships are powerful. When we sit and listen to people's stories and what God is doing in their lives, God becomes more real, and we begin to ask God to be that big in our life back at home or ask, "God how can you use me back at home to serve and love my neighbors?" Getting caught in the trap of needing to get the project done or needing to "save" someone means you'll miss God in the people around you and you'll miss the seeds of faith that'll grow long after the trip.

Pictures, stories, and reminders can help our people continue on the journey toward Jesus. The more we remember, the longer it will stay with us. And as the trip leaders maintain relationships with the community the team visited, we can give updates and prayer requests of the ministries and people we met while on the trip, reminding us of the people we met, what we learned, what we committed, and keeping our faith growing.

Overcoming Power Differences Through Relationships

At the root of so many of the issues and complexities of short-term missions is the inescapable power difference between visiting groups and the communities they work within. But acknowledging the difference and investing in reciprocal relationships can do a lot to diffuse the damage the power difference could cause.

Whether we like it or not, when we as American mission trip participants step into a community that is in need, we are the ones who hold the power. No matter what posture we take, there is an automatic power difference. Due to the perception of America around the world, good or bad, there is an expectation that we have money and resources. Therefore host communities take the posture of humility, not wanting to offend us, many times submitting their will and agenda to ours. We have the financial backing of a church. We have participants with expendable income.

We have the power to either make a meaningful difference or do incredible damage. What we do with this power matters to Jesus, and Jesus provided the example for how to humbly use our power. Here's how Paul describes Christ in Philippians 2, with my asides about following Christ's example:

Do nothing out of selfish ambition or vain conceit.
(How often have our short-term mission trips been about our selfish, church-centric ambition?)

Rather, in humility
(Humility is not thinking less of yourself; it's not thinking of yourself at all.)

value others above yourselves,
(Let us put our preferences for our church, youth group, and trip participants to the side.)

not looking to your own interests but each of you to the interests of the others.

Reciprocal Missions

(This is the reciprocal part. What if both the mission trip group and host spent time looking into the interests of the other and found a way to do the work together?)

In your relationships with one another
(There is that darn word again, *relationships*.)

have the same mindset as Christ Jesus:
(*Mindset* is what we know to be true in our gut and living it out in deeds. To be Christ-like, to live like He lived.)

Who, being in the very nature God, did not consider equality with God something to be used to his own advantage;
(What if we rewrite this for ourselves? "Who, being an American, did not consider his privilege as an American something to be used to his own advantage.")

rather, he made himself nothing by taking the very nature of a servant, being made in human likeness.

Jesus, the Creator of the universe, did not consider His privilege as God as something to be used to His own advantage. Jesus stepped into our cold, dark, broken world and used His power for the benefit of those on the underside of life—the poor, displaced, marginalized, abused, oppressed, and kicked to the curb. Jesus humbled Himself, and when someone asked to be healed, He never turned them away. He used His power to stand up against the religious, oppressive authority of His day. Jesus lived with and walked with the outcasts of His day. He listened to their needs, their pain, and their heartache, and He understood what they needed. Jesus gave His power away to those in need by humbling Himself and setting them free.

The American church needs humility when we enter into short-term mission trips. We simply can't develop reciprocal relationships when one side has power they're unwilling to give up. When we let go of our power so others can flourish, we're able to receive from them the deep insights they have into their community and their real need.

How do we humble ourselves and navigate the power difference? When we at Be2Live begin developing a new ministry partner, we don't do anything significant with the ministry for at least the first year. We typically prepare a meal and do some on-site maintenance, whatever small, often unseen task that helps the organization and builds our relationship. But our primary focus is the relationship. We want to get to know the orphanage director, the pastor, the ministry leader, the volunteers, and the community. We want to hear their stories and understand what their true needs are. We do not want to make any assumptions, and we want to provide a safe place for them to share where it hurts. It takes time, and sometimes it's a painful process, and it doesn't look glamorous, but it is worth it.

Over time and through the posture of humility, we can create shared goals for our groups and the host organization. Talk to the host, find out what is needed, and discuss how your team can best meet the needs of the community. Be open with your hopes and be willing to adapt them to the feedback and insights of the host. Expect to have to ask more than once to get the full picture of their true needs, from our experience and research, few hosting ministries have groups that care more about the organization they are serving than their trip outcomes. As you proceed, communicate the goals to everyone involved, and keep the shared goals at the center of every part of the trip.

When we are humble and available, we will not only avoid making a negative impact, we will develop reciprocal relationships that have the potential to change lives and communities for the long haul. How cool is that!

.

DJ's 2 Cents

Much of the harm done in short-term missions can be summed up in a lack of humility. The battle between pride and humility is ongoing in all of our lives and is the base for all of our struggles. We might think we're humble, but the paradox is if we think we're humble, we're not. This will be obvious to everyone you encounter on your mission trip.

To truly be self-aware is incredibly difficult. It's almost impossible to truly understand how we are perceived by those around us and what kind of impact we are having either positively or negatively. It's even harder when we're serving in a culture that is foreign to us.

The need for honesty with yourself, and honest input from your on-the-ground host is critical. This is why it's crucial to build an ongoing relationship in your destination country. Without some history and trust being built with a relationship, honesty can be kind of rare. Most hosts would never criticize the visiting team for fear of offending, but it's only when we're truly honest with each other that healthy reciprocal relationships are built. We need to build trust between the host and team leaders so we can be truly honest and transparent with each other. We need to have intentional conversations with everyone involved, showing our hearts and our true desire to serve each other. With honest input, received in a humble fashion, your mission experience will grow deeper and more impactful over time. Short-term missions should be done well, and doing things well takes research, practice, and honest coaching over time.

CHAPTER 4

Saving the Church in America

DJ

Missions relationships should be reciprocal, a blessing to all involved. But so far, we've focused largely on how trips can best be beneficial to the communities being served. This chapter is all about what's in it for the visiting teams. What teams experience is vital for the dire struggles the American church is facing.

So often, short-term mission team members say to us in the field, "I'm leaving with so much more than I came with." Obviously they're not talking about material wealth; they're leaving with something much more valuable. The teams are leaving with a greater worldview and, more importantly, a renewed and energized faith—which in many ways is more valuable than any skills, supplies, or financing they might have brought to their destination countries.

Americans face an ever-growing number of distractions, and many in the church even consider them false gods or idols, which I'm unsure about, but the risks are real. When church is considered just another distraction, does sports, hunting, working out, or endless hours online take the place of God? We all want a nest egg, but when does our desire for financial security begin to take the place of our God? How many people today wrap their limited church attendance around their children's sports schedules? What is that teaching our children about making church and God priority?

There are more false idols today than ever before, and they are getting more powerful as they cry out for our attention. It's common to see people on their phones during church checking social media. The world seems to be spinning faster and faster, and as technology increases there are more and more demands on the few precious hours we have available. How can the church compete with all the interests vying for our time, attention, and involvement? How do you break through the noise? The default reaction is to make the church as "friendly" as possible by adding more coffee houses, spending more on worship, and remodeling the stage to be as Pinterest friendly as possible. Almost any pastime can now come under the mantle of the church if it keeps people's interests: golf, knitting, surfing, or yoga "ministries" and even church micro-brew pubs.

The church in America is in a sad state. Attendance is plummeting, and those who do show up do so as a cultural experience or family tradition, not primarily to seek God. As older church members die, younger people aren't filling their places. Fewer millennials attend church on a regular basis than any prior generation, and the fastest growing belief system in the U.S. today is atheism[8]. Churches have been battling the trend of departing youth for a very long time. In generations past, the youth would eventually come back to church, but the millennial generation, at least so far, seem less apt to return.

Oddly, one theory of why the church is dying in America is that it has become too easy. There is no sacrifice or true commitment required. As long as people show up, it's all good. There is no commitment or change of lifestyle required. There is a much higher level of

[8] http://www.pewforum.org/2015/05/12/americas-changing-religious-landscape/

commitment required to join a high school football team or a youth soccer league. God does welcome us as we are with open arms, but then He asks for commitment, sacrifice, and our working to take on more of His image. I spoke to one pastor of a large church in Southern California, and he shared that they consider someone a "church member" if they attend once every 6 weeks. Other than semi-regular attendance and tithing, what does the church in America require of us?

In writing this book I took the opportunity to speak with a wide range of missionaries and people who host mission groups from the U.S.. We covered a broad range of topics and questions, but the unifying theme I found was a general contempt for the church in America. There was an overall feeling that the vast majority of the church in America just didn't get it. The church in America is concerning themselves with being polite, well organized, and well dressed while people are dying all around them, literally and spiritually. My goal is not to offend people, but to help each of us see that change is needed in order for the church to thrive.

So, with this bleak outlook or opinion of the local church, what's the answer? It's impossible to compete with the hectic world we live in; it's silly for the church to even try.

It may help to look at where in the world the church is thriving and doing well. The Gospel is spreading in majority countries and areas of the world most at risk. In Cuba, China, in any country where the church is under true persecution, the church thrives. Historically, the church thrives in persecution—and the pushback the church in America gets is nothing compared to the persecution around the world and throughout history. In countries where people are struggling financially and living at a level of poverty we can hardly imagine, they know what it means to depend on God. In areas where the distractions of the world are not as accessible, people can spend time with God and really listen to His will.

So are poverty and persecution the answer for the American church? We all grow from trials, from storms, from the attacks that come. Maybe the church in America has had it too easy for too long and is now in a weak and dying state. Any living thing grows and thrives with healthy challenges. If any living thing is overfed and becomes too comfortable, atrophy sets in and it begins to die. We could say the church in America needs more persecution or to give up its wealth, but at least in the short-term that is not going to happen (and it's an odd thing to hope for).

I believe short-term missions can save the church. When people come into contact with poverty and persecution that others face and see how faith thrives in the face of difficulty, they will be changed. And they can bring that desperately needed change back to their homes and churches.

The standard model for missions is: "Let's go and tell that group of people over there about the Gospel." It might be time for us to discuss flipping that model to: "Let's go over there and experience the level of faith we have a hard time finding at home." Maybe, just maybe, if we go out with an open mind, something different might happen. If we go out with the attitude of: "Yes, we're here to serve, but what can I learn from these people who are so on fire for God?" What are people doing well in other parts of the world that we can bring home?

As travel became safer, faster, and more economical than it's ever been before, it's made it exponentially easier to send small teams to almost anywhere in the world on short-term trips. And maybe that's just what the church needs. Below are 7 ways that short-term missions can help to save the church.

Spending Time With People Who Inspire

Years ago, before vaccinations, if a child had chickenpox, it was common for the moms in the area to get together and have all the kids hang out so they could infect each other (since it's much better to have chickenpox as a child than later as an adult). Faith acts the same way—it's easy to catch when you're around someone who's infected. (And, it seems, it can have a particular effect on young people.) We can read about it, be preached at, maybe even be exposed to it through family history or tradition, yet until we hang out with someone who is truly passionate about their faith, someone who has been infected by their experience with Jesus, it's hard for our faith to become real and personal to us.

I'm assuming if you're reading this book you are a believer who has come to a real relationship with Jesus Christ. You have secured your salvation and are now living to serve Him wherever He might call you. If you are like the vast majority of believers, you were first drawn to the faith by spending time with someone else who was passionate about their faith and their walk with Jesus. This is truly how things spread, one-on-one and relationally. Even if you came to the Lord at a large concert or outreach, odds are you were invited by someone else who had already experienced the joy of walking with Jesus. Can faith sprout spontaneously when someone is reading by themselves or just spending time contemplating the Lord? Absolutely. But it is much more likely to be spread by contact with another believer.

Relationships change us. They inspire us. They give us life. They spark our faith and help it grow. We need to find ways to bump up against people who inspire us, who encourage us to reach for greatness in all we attempt. We need to find people to set an example of faith in our lives.

Short-term missions makes these kinds of relationships possible. In missions, relationships are everything. Traditionally a missionary would move to an area and spend years building relationships in an attempt to influence people and share the faith. On a short-term mission trip, by definition, the relationships are shorter, but they don't have to end. By returning again and again to the same people and area over the course of years, you can build long-term relationships that are reciprocal and healthy. With the advent of social media, it's easier to keep up with others around the world, so the influence, in both directions, does not have to end when you head home.

A few years back I was on a small team putting together the curriculum for a 30-day mission training program. We were assembling themes, speakers, and activities for a group of fifteen or so college students joining us for the program. Someone on the planning team made a comment that stuck with me: "The topics are important, but what the students will remember are the inspirational people they get to spend time with."

Certainly a teacher, a coach, a boss, friend, or a family member can inspire us to be a better version of ourselves, but the dynamic experience of traveling on short-term mission trips seems to create those opportunities to be inspired by others. Once we leave our home country, it's easier to spend time with people who face hardship, who've experienced a defining moment that changed their lives. You can meet people from other cultures who live in vastly different situations. You can meet missionaries, nurses, doctors, construction workers, and others who've decided to dedicate a period of their lives to the neediest and the most hurting.

I want to tell you about Dave. In 2009 Dave was just another normal middle-aged man from Northern California. He had no ministry training, and had never worked full-time with a ministry; he was just an average guy who took a chance on a short-term mission trip. I don't think Dave was expecting a whole lot when he signed up. On the trip, he met some people in Baja, Mexico serving the poorest of the poor in the dump area of Tijuana. Six months after his mission trip, he walked away from what he had in the U.S. and found his new life serving the children and families living in pallet houses in Tijuana. Today this guy glows—glows with a joy that few people ever experience. He never complains, never loses hope, and trusts completely in God. He was inspired by God through his interaction with a few people doing great things, and now Dave is that inspiration to others.

I love sending people to "help" Dave. Dave doesn't need any help. The people I send to him are the ones who need inspiration, who need their lives changed, who need their worlds rocked. They need what Dave has and the transformation he experienced.

I want to point out a couple of things about the example of Dave you just read. Although Dave was active in his local church in California, it took a short-term mission trip to really set his faith on fire.

He was surrounded by good people at home, and obviously God can work on someone anywhere, but that one week where he took a chance and left the country to see how God could use him dramatically changed his life. Not everyone will go into missions full-time, but some will, and some lives will change in other ways as they return home.

Inspiring people can be found almost anywhere, but in my limited experience, they're easier to find where life is harder, where life is more of a struggle than we typically experience in the U.S. In Ghana, Peru, and Mexico, you can encounter people of extreme faith—and we tend to be more receptive to relationships when we're far from where we're comfortable.

So do we organize and plan mission trips just so we can meet giants of the faith? No. But we need to realize that meeting with inspiring people is just one of the many benefits of short-term missions. We all have something to offer, and teams from the U.S. bring greatly needed talents and resources to the majority of countries they are traveling out to. It truly is a reciprocal relationship.

Giving the Church a Rallying Point

Short-term missions benefit the church as a whole, not just through the transformed lives of individuals. They give groups of believers a goal to work toward together. We all need goals in our lives or we can tend to stagnate, where we're just going through the motions in our day-to-day. It's healthy psychologically and emotionally to have something we're moving toward, whether it's finishing our degree, saving to buy a house, or writing a book.

When done right, preparing for, and supporting, a short-term mission trip can galvanize a church into action. Even more so if they build a solid, healthy, ongoing relationship with a mission or missionary. The act of "sender" is critical; it's not just about funding. The church, or at least a team at the church, needs to show they support the mission team with prayer and emotional support, being excited about what God has laid out for them and the people they are traveling to.

Several years ago one of the older boys in our orphanage came to me and told me his eye was bothering him. We made an appointment to have him checked out, but within 24 hours he had lost all sight in that one eye. As we moved from specialist to specialist, it was determined that he had a golf-ball-sized tumor that was growing and crushing his optic nerve. As we worked to get him to a specialist in the U.S., something powerful happened. We operate as a large Christian family, and prayer is part of our daily lives, but this challenge really upped it a notch or two. Without any coaching from us, our children started a voluntary dawn prayer meeting. Churches from across Mexico and the U.S. began praying for him and the situation. A few miracles later, he had a passport, medical visa, and an appointment in the U.S. with one of the top neurosurgeons in California. On the day before he was scheduled to leave, we had a soccer game here on site with a bunch of the local teens to send him off. Without any prompting from us, the soccer teams (made up mainly of nonbelievers) formed a circle around him to pray him off. After several surgeries, he is now doing fine, attending college, and waiting tables to earn spending money.

God used that cancer to create an incredible sense of unity here in the home and brought our level of prayer to new heights. God used this illness to give our home a rallying point, something for everyone to focus on and work toward solving. It took our eyes off our own problems and focused them on something bigger.

You might have experienced a general focusing and rallying in your own church. It might be a building fund that brings the conversation and efforts of everyone into focus. Missions, when done in a healthy way, can become a rallying point, something everyone wants to work toward.

Many churches have been transformed by their involvement in short-term missions. There is a church in the middle of Iowa that sends two teams of 60 people to Mexico every year. It's become such a rallying point for the church that when they open sign-ups online, it normally sells out within 30 minutes and they have to start a wait-ing list. I was speaking at one church that works with us, and as a way of introduction the pastor asked for everyone who had been on a mission trip to stand up. Out of a church of roughly 400 people, 300 of them have been actively involved in short-term missions. I know a church of about 600 outside of Seattle that has been very faithful in supporting their high school short-term mission trips. The team hosts a dinner fundraiser every year and roughly 2/3 of the church shows up to eat dinner, donate to the cause, and show their support.

I'm not saying you set up a mission table at your church's en-trance and suddenly people will be falling over themselves to join, but it can be a starting point. If a lead pastor is behind a mission project or, even better, commits to going on the trip the first year or two, it can begin to create some powerful conversations within the church.

Building Church Unity

Church unity is subtly different than giving the church a rallying point. Building unity in the body of Christ can be difficult in the hec-tic world we live in with all of its distractions. The believers coming together as one to support and build up one another is fundamental to our faith.

It's hard to really get to know somebody on a typical Sunday morning church service. It's a little easier to get to know somebody if you attend a Bible study or class together. When you're serving alongside someone you start to get to know them and their true cha-racter. If you really want to get to know someone, travel with them, be put in uncomfortable situations together, and face each other be-fore you've had coffee in the morning. There is no better bonding for a team of high school students, young adults, or older adults than living together 24 hours a day for a week or two. Building a house together, completing a well-drilling project, or just sitting around a campfire debriefing about the day's events allows people to truly get to know each other.

If the short-term leader understands this dynamic, they can use a trip to create bonding memories that will join the team emotionally for years to come. Just by sitting around a table late at night and throwing the right questions out to encourage the team to share, it allows the team members time to open up about their observations, feelings, and reactions to the various events of the day. It allows them to talk about their reaction to physical poverty; it allows them to open up about the joys and pains they might have seen in the people they were interacting with; it allows them to be real with each other. We all know this does not happen at that depth very often in this world.

Teaching the Church to Serve

I cynically opened up this chapter by generally referring to the church in America as a spectator sport. I sincerely hope I am wrong in my opinions because our faith is so much more than just attaining salvation and spending the rest of our lives hidden away in a museum for Christians. We are called to be active in our faith, to be a light unto the world, to be used by God to change lives. Stop right here and ask yourself if the majority of the people in your church are truly focused on representing Jesus well, if they are actively serving others.

One of the many attributes of Christ is service. Jesus spent the bulk of His time focused on those around Him. He spent His time healing, teaching, encouraging, feeding, blessing whenever He came into contact with others. During the last supper, the last night He had with the apostles, Jesus could have taught on anything. He chose feet washing, an example of service with profound symbolism at that time; it was the lowest servants who would perform this act for others. Jesus felt it was significant to close out His training with the apostles by giving them this deep, powerful example of service.

If we call ourselves followers of Christ yet are not actively, humbly serving others in our day-to-day lives, we are hypocrites.

If your church has an active and enthusiastic culture of service, praise God! If your church pays lip service to the importance of service and reaching out to others, you might have some work to do. For Christians to be healthy they have to be serving others. There is no way around this. There is need all around us to be addressed, but we should also be serving because it's emotionally healthy for us, and it should be a natural response of thanksgiving for our incredible gift of salvation.

Serving the people within the walls of your church is a good thing—serving people and sharing the Gospel with those in your surrounding area is even better. By sending teams on short-term missions you will allow them to experience the joys of service at a different level and address much greater physical needs than you would probably encounter in your own town. Also, when teams serve locally it is typically for a few hours or maybe for a weekend; by sending a team for a week or two they are able to have a greater understanding of what it means to lead a life of service. They get to experience on a deeper level the Christian paradox that the more we open ourselves up to others, serve others, and give of ourselves, the greater the joy. As we take our eyes off ourselves and our own problems and challenges, we are able to focus more on those around us and what is truly a priority in this life. Teaching your church the joys of walking like Jesus can be the second greatest gift you share beyond salvation.

Learning to Trust in God's Protection

"Isn't Mexico dangerous?" I can't tell you how many times I've had to respond to this question over the last 20 years. I honestly believe this is more of a statement on the church in America today than any perceived danger in Mexico.

Way too many people live lives wrapped in fear of things that don't happen or don't matter. American culture feeds and encourages fear: fear of the other political party, of terrorists, of people from different countries or cultures. Fear has become the new American way and is way too common in churches. Avoiding liability trumps trusting in God almost across the board.

A few years ago I got a phone call from a concerned father who was looking at sending his daughter with their church mission team to serve with our orphanage in Mexico. After talking to him for a while, he asked me straight out: "Can you 100% guarantee the safety of my daughter?" I think I surprised him with my answer: "Absolutely not." I asked him if he could 100% guarantee the safety of his daughter when she was driving to school, out shopping, or even in their home. There are almost no 100% guarantees in this life other than the fact that we will all eventually die. If we lived our lives looking for 100% guarantees, we would never do anything. That's not why we're on this earth.

At what point did the church collectively decide that we need complete security at all times? Why are we so afraid? Jesus never taught that we should only go and share the Gospel if our safety could be guaranteed, that we should only help others if there is zero risk involved. I'm not saying we should take unnecessary chances, but what should we be willing to risk to share the Gospel?

In 2014 my wife and I were scheduled to travel with a team of about 20 to Ghana in West Africa. We had our tickets, we had our visas, and about 30 days before we were scheduled to leave, the Ebola outbreak hit West Africa. You couldn't pick up a paper, turn on the radio, or watch the news without being told how dangerous Ebola was and how we were all going to die. Not the best time to travel to West Africa. Over the course of a few weeks, most of the team dropped out, and, to be honest, we thought about it. We made a few calls to people on the ground to get accurate information and had some *long* talks. Any sane person would have canceled (though we've never been grouped in with sane people). We decided to go. The team was just five people, and *everyone* said we were crazy. But West Africa is a big place, and where we were serving was over 1,000 miles from the nearest Ebola case. At no time were we in any danger, other than malaria and the other normal issues from that area. We had an incredible trip, and I believe we had a real impact at the orphanage where we were serving.

In looking back at our trip to Ghana, I'm flooded with emotions. One of the emotions I have is regret for the many people who, out of an abundance of caution, chose not to go. They missed out on a life-changing experience. They missed out on the chance to share with others and connect with believers on the other side of the world. The enemy, once again, used fear to stop ministry from taking place. Who knows what our impact could've been?

"Fear not" comes up a lot in the Bible, but "You need to avoid risk" isn't mention explicitly or implicitly. If we believe we have an all powerful, loving Father in Heaven who only wants what's best for us, why are we so afraid? The church needs to learn to trust in God, and the best way to do that is step out and practice this trust, to experience this trust, to let God show you it's going to be OK. Help your church to take some chances. Go drill a well in Kenya, go build a house in Baja, and your church will be better for it.

Losing American Exceptionalism

It's easy to feel that "America knows how to do it better." Despite that attitude bombarding us, the evidence is clear: America doesn't have it all figured out and can't solve the world's problems. Going on a short-term mission trip makes this abundantly clear.

There are a lot of ways to judge a country. I am an American, and I'm proud to be an American, but I also understand America doesn't have all the answers. In many basic areas we rank way down the list worldwide: infant mortality rate, income discrepancies, math and science education, healthcare, etc. Pretty much the only area where we consistently rate in the top three worldwide is obesity.

In our day-to-day lives if we attend the same church, go to the same job, hang out with more or less the same people, even visit the same websites every day, it's easy to live in our own little bubble. If we only spend time with people who look, think, and act a lot like us, it's very hard to have a view of humanity as a whole. Even if we regularly read or watch international news, what's portrayed in any media outlet is frequently skewed in one direction or another. Until we get out and meet people in other areas, walk the streets of a foreign city, watch the news about America from a different country, it can be hard to truly understand the bigger world and how it interacts and functions.

Spending Time With the Body of Christ

We've covered a lot of ways short-term missions could impact the church in America. I believe we've saved the most important point for last. Short-term missions allow us to spend time with churches that are on fire, that are going through revival, churches that are passionately in love with Jesus.

Around the world God is doing incredible work through financially poor, persecuted, understaffed churches. Standing in a church in the middle of Ghana you can experience a level of real, joyful worship that makes anything you can experience in a U.S. megachurch pale in comparison. In a cramped living room in Cuba listening to an "uneducated" pastor preach the Gospel makes the best trained theologian sound dry and feeble. Hearing the stories of pure joy experienced by persecuted American missionaries in a Muslim country makes the writings of Paul come alive. The church in America is in desperate need of experiencing faith as a child, faith that is all consuming, faith as God intended our relationship with Him to be.

In our own lives, we become like the people we hang out with. If we hang out with people who eat too much, we will eat too much. If we hang out with people who exercise, we will exercise more. If we hang out with people who are cynical and sarcastic, those traits will grow in our own lives. Faith works in the same way. If we spend time with people who are passionate about their walk with Jesus and are truly living it out, we will be drawn to do the same. If our church spends time with and builds relationships with churches experiencing revival, with churches trusting in God at a deeper level, our church will be healthier. Even in our areas of health, churches in different situations and cultures live out their faith differently, and that experience can enrich us and help us grow. Christ's body is full of variety, and we all need each other to survive.

Phil's 2 Cents

If you are paying attention to the American church, you know full well that we are losing people like no other time in history. I want to propose another way of reaching people through short-term missions and bringing them back to church.

One of the biggest reasons people have left the church, especially the evangelical church, is because they feel as though the church does not care about the poor, orphan, immigrant, refugee, and marginalized in our country or in our world. They see a church paying lip service, but not doing anything real and tangible about these issues. They want to see a church that concerns themselves with justice and joining God in restoring the world and making things right.

People today want to know if God cares about the social issues facing our world today. A person would have to be heartless to not care about orphans, slavery, poverty, or those marginalized in our world. Whenever I share with people who are outside the church what we are doing on our short-term mission trips, learning and getting involved in fighting the injustices in our world today, they want to know more and how they can get involved. If people see a church actively engaging in these social issues and going to places where these things are happening, they will be more inclined to join you in the cause. Why not use the short-term mission trip as a way to reach people through God's heart for the marginalized?

The majority of the students (90%) who participate on our short-term mission trips are nonbelievers or don't go to church anywhere. Yes, it is messy. Yes, we need to tell them that they can't say certain things on a trip. But wow—these students come face-to-face with a God who cares about the things and people they care about. They begin to see and understand a God they had no idea existed. They hear stories from people who are pillars in their faith, and they see God in real and tangible ways, and their lives are forever changed.

CHAPTER 5

Developing the Right Motivations

Phil

"Most youth pastors, outreach pastors, or others who lead short-term mission trips just don't care." These unsettling words were said by the director of a ministry in a conversation we were having about the effects of short-term missions on his ministry. He's not the only one who feels this way. Though he's seen the positive impact of some groups, he's seen many who are a tremendous burden, damaging the ministry and the community.

It all comes down to our motivations for short-term missions. Our actions and words reveal why we lead and go on these trips. How we treat the ministry and the communities we visit, our requests, demands, and actions reveal why we are there. So we need to stop and take a serious look at why we go on and lead these trips. Why are we going on a short-term mission trip? Why are you, the leader, taking your students or team on a short-term mission trip? Understanding our motivations will determine how we interact with the people we go to serve with and the success or failure of the trip and whether we will do damage to the host community or make a positive difference.

As leaders of a short-term mission team, it is our responsibility to clearly define our "why" and communicate our motivation to everyone else on our trip, at our church, and our supporters. Before we do any planning, buying airline tickets and forming our team, we as leaders must define why we are going. Our "why's" will probably change as we move through the trip as we have new experiences, meet new people, and God reveals Himself to us. But as long as we are seeking reciprocal humble relationships with those we are serving, our motivations will be in the right place.

There are many reasons why people initially sign up to go on a short-term mission trip, but leaders must do the hard work of helping everyone understand why we are going. Some of the reasons I have heard are:

"I am following Jesus' call to go into all the world and preach the Gospel."

"I want to go serve and love others."

"I want to be more grateful for what I have."

"I'm going because I don't think it's safe for my daughter to go on the mission trip by herself."

"I want to share my testimony with someone who needs it."

"I just need service hours to graduate."

"I want to learn about another culture."

Now, these aren't all bad reasons, but are they what we want for our teams? More importantly, is it what the host community or ministry wants from us? Even if our initial reasons for going are out of a good and pure heart, we must be willing to be challenged in our motivations.

Motivations Are Complicated

When I meet missionaries or directors of NGOs (non-governmental organizations) in other countries, I am always interested in what they honestly think of short-term mission groups. Since I lead an organization that has taken thousands of people on short-term mission trips, I realize it might be an awkward question to answer. Knowing that I don't know what I don't know, realizing sometimes we have blown it, and with a deep desire to reframe how short-term missions has been done, I don't settle for the first answer. Many times I know there are deeper issues that are not first mentioned.

I recently visited a missionary in Thailand to learn about his ministry of reaching marginalized people. I was also interested in learning about how Be2Live could partner with them in supporting their work. As we spent the week together and our relationship was built, the missionary shared a story with me.

This missionary had been hosting a medical team of doctors for a number of years. They would come and see many patients in the northern part of Thailand. These well-meaning doctors were doing good work in treating the sick and meeting people's needs. The government came to the missionary and asked him to ask the doctors to do two things: Stop issuing these "exotic" medicines that they don't have in Thailand because they were unable to refill the prescriptions after they ran out. More importantly, the government asked the American doctors to train the Thailand doctors so that they could more sufficiently meet their own people's needs. To the missionary's surprise, the American doctors refused to train the local doctors. A request like this, although complicated, would have a lasting impact. The following year the doctors stopped coming.

What did the actions of the doctors reveal about their motivations and their heart for the Thai people? Who was this short-term medical trip really for?

The missionary then told me, "People want to save the world, but they don't want to save Thailand." What a profound statement! We can substitute any country, city, or community: "People want to save the world, but they don't want to save Mexico." "People want to save the world, but they don't want to save Chicago." It's more glamorous and exciting to "save the world" than it is do the hard work of eradicating one issue in one place over the long haul.

Our true motivation is revealed through our actions, words, and thoughts while we are in the moment on the trip. How do we respond to the host when they tell us, "No, we don't want you to do that" or if they ask us to do something different than what we planned? To complicate things even more, as the week goes on and we get more tired, our margins shrink. We can know our true motives by looking at our thoughts, actions, and words:

- Are we complaining about the cold showers, food, or living conditions of our team?

- Are we refusing to comply with the orphanage, ministry, or community's dress code?

- Are we making noise in the housing area past quiet time?

- Do we care about the quality of our work?

- Are we honoring local customs, laws, and relationships?

- Are we allowing the host community leader to lead our team?

- Do we devalue the work of the locals because it is not how we would do it in the United States?

We need to be honest with ourselves and check both our conscious and unconscious motivations. Conscious motivations are the ones we talk about and give us reason for going. Unconscious motivations are the ones below the surface, and many times we don't know they are there. If we are not honest with ourselves and our teams, we can do more damage than good. As fallen human beings it is hard for us to approach everything with pure motives. We aren't always going to get it right, but if we examine ourselves, invite God to help us, and allow the relationships we form to challenge and change us, we can grow in our motivations, our impact, and our relationship with God.

With every motivation there is the potential of an unconscious motivation alongside. We need to be aware of these as we go on our trips. Let's take a look at some conscious and corresponding unconscious motivations.

Conscious Motivation #1:
"We're going to preach the Gospel so that we can save people's lives."

We may use the following verses to answer our why:

- "Go and make disciples of all nations, baptizing them in the name of the Father and of the Son and of the Holy Spirit" (Matthew 28:19).

- "Go into all the world and preach the gospel to all nations" (Mark 16:15).

- "But you will receive power when the Holy Spirit comes on you; and you will be my witnesses in Jerusalem, and in all Judea and Samaria, and to the ends of the earth" (Acts 1:8).

For some, our conscious motivation is to go and fulfill the great commission. This is a worthy calling—but if we are honest with ourselves, is it best accomplished on a short-term trip? The Gospel message is vital, but are our methods most effective? Is it best for our short-term mission teams to go into other communities to "preach the Gospel," performing skits in the park, asking for decisions, without having a growing relationship or a follow-up plan? If your host church is asking you to help put on an outreach, and they have people prepared to follow up with others long after your team leaves, then join them.

My years as a Campus Life Director in Northeast Indiana taught me the importance of relational ministry. Many of us approach ministry by building relationships with people who are far from Christ in hopes of "earning the right to be heard" so that you can share your relationship with Jesus with them. Usually these relationships take months, if not years to develop. If this is the case for us back at home with neighbors and coworkers we so often see, then should we not apply this same reasoning to our short-term mission trips? If we as a church or organization teach relational ministry to our students, adult volunteers, and congregation but don't practice it on our short-term mission trips, then we are hypocrites.

The majority of the high school students we take on our service and learning trips are nonbelievers or students who have little to no faith or church background. On one of our summer trips, we were working with a ministry partner in town while they were doing an outreach event to the community. Along with our group was a group of American Christian doctors and nurses who were performing medical exams and meeting the physical needs of the people in the community. Our students were asked to do arts and crafts with the children while they waited to see the doctor.

When one of the American nurses learned that our students were not believers, this nurse was intent on leading one of them to Christ. At lunch, the nurse cornered one of our students and began trying to evangelize, peppering the student with questions and pleading her case for the "Gospel." Let me remind you this student had never met this nurse.

Eventually our student relented and said the prayer of salvation. The nurse went away rejoicing that she had led a student to the Lord, never to see or follow up with her again. After this interaction, they both had two very different stories of what happened.

The nurse relayed how she had led one of our students to the Lord and how excited she was that she was able to do this! Our student's response was completely different. "I could not get out of the conversation, so I repeated after her some prayer so I could be done. I have no idea what I said."

This is not a responsible way of sharing the Gospel. But this was someone's idea that they were called to share the Gospel with no follow-up or relationship with the person. This is not what God intended for us to do with the Good News.

If you are partnering with a church or ministry and they ask you to do a salvation skit or to present the Gospel—if it was their idea and their direction—then by all means, proceed. If while on a short-term mission trip you feel as though God is leading you to share the Gospel with someone, then by all means, do so. But let us bathe each nudge by the Holy Spirit in prayer before we step out and attempt as best we can to connect the person we're sharing with to a person or ministry who will be there long-term to help them grow in Christ.

Unconscious Motivation #1:
"We need to validate the cost of the short-term mission trip."

During my time at a previous Christian organization in Indiana, I had to sit down and fill out my weekly ministry report and turn it into my supervisor. On this ministry report, I had to write down what I did for the week and what the results were. How many students came to club that week? How many building times and appointments did I have that week? But it was known that the most requested stat was, "How many times did you present the Gospel and how many students made decisions?" We knew that every week we were expected to "present the Gospel" to students whether through one on one appointments or at our clubs. The number of presentations and decisions was also important as it related to our parent organization chapter as well as our prayer letters we sent out on a monthly basis.

Now don't get me wrong, I am all for sharing Jesus with as many people as possible. But when we boil the Gospel down to a number and an expectation of decisions made, then we are not being responsible with the Gospel. Nor am I sure that we are being responsible with the relationship. It is far too easy to see a person as a project to be saved over getting to know them and genuinely caring for them, just as they are. Jesus did this so well. He saw the individual and met them where they were. I wanted as many students as possible to make decisions to following Jesus, but if part of my job was about the number of decisions being made, what was my true motivation for presenting the Gospel? Yes, it was for students to know, love, and follow Jesus, but to say that my motives were completely pure would not be true. Many times it seemed as though my motivation for presenting the Gospel was more about me and my ministry report and prayer letters than it was actually about being sensitive to the Holy Spirit. My unconscious motivation was so that I looked good in doing my ministry. It made me feel better about myself and my ministry.

There are many churches today who go on short-term mission trips with the expressed purpose of "presenting the Gospel." But we must be willing to dig deeper into our motivations and consider the following questions: Why do we do Gospel presentations? Is it so that we can report back to our church how many decisions were made for Christ so that we can validate that our trip was worth the cost?

If the Gospel is our priority, there are many questions to consider: What if there was a different way of presenting the Gospel? What if we help provide for a church so that they can be more effective in presenting the Gospel to their community? What if we were able to give what is needed to churches to reach their community in the way they feel is best? Can we develop a sister church in the community with a long-term ministry relationship that celebrates with each other, prays for each other, and ministers to each other?

Let's periodically check ourselves and keep working toward the bigger long-term impact that can be had when our churches invest in indigenous churches to reach their community.

Conscious Motivation #2:
"We are going to sacrifice for those we are serving."

When people go on short-term mission trips, many sacrifice their vacation time, money, and time with family. Others spend a lot of time and energy raising money for their trip. Many groups go knowing that their living conditions will be less than comfortable. People go willingly to sleep in bunk houses, eat new and different foods that might make them sick, and not take a shower for a week. They are willing to sacrifice the comforts of home so that they can work with those in the community they are serving.

Unconscious Motivation #2:
"I'll serve others as long as my needs are met."

Though we intend to sacrifice and willingly give up the comforts of home, many times this just doesn't play out on the trip. When the rubber meets the road, we revert to our perceived need of our creature comforts, sometimes without even realizing it.

An orphanage in Latin America had a housing facility for its short-term mission teams where it had five showers for the group. But the showers had little water pressure, making it hard to take a "good" shower and get the soap out of their hair. The housing facility shared the same water source as the rest of the orphanage. After a few days of subpar showers, the group leader asked the orphanage staff if they could turn off the water to the children in the orphanage between 3:00-5:00 p.m. so their team could take a shower with good water pressure. Though this mission team came with good intentions, when they felt uncomfortable and dirty, their motivation turned from serving others to serving their needs.

When we enter into the communities we are serving, let us be aware of how people are living around us. Yes, it would be nice to have hot showers with strong water pressure. Trust me, I like to feel clean and fresh every day, but not at the expense of someone who has less than me on a daily basis and especially those I am serving with in the community. (Many people living in the community didn't even have a shower, let alone hot water.) My needs are not as important as those I am serving. If we pause to consider the norms of the community we are serving in, it might surprise us to see how nice our mission trip housing really is and help us to sacrifice the comforts of home for the week.

When you are on your mission trip, what requests or demands are you making of the host organization? Are you asking for more than what the host or community has access to on a daily basis?

Conscious Motivation #3:
"Let's get the job done!"

This is another service-oriented goal. Over the years we have had groups, mainly adults, who want to know what the project is and will work to get it done at all costs; even if it means they need to skip dinner or even "tourist" day off. I love groups like this that want to get work done. Many host organizations have gotten so efficient in their house building that you can build a house in four days. Other organizations know what projects they would like you to do, whether repairing a house, building a church, or adding on a room.

How often do we go on a short-term mission trip with a project we want to accomplish in one week? We like seeing our progress, and we want to honor our commitment to the churches and supporters who have helped pay for not only our trip but also for the project we are doing. It is a good thing when we come with the motivation of wanting to use our gifts, talents, or grunt labor on a work site to get the job done. But what is the possible unconscious motivation?

Unconscious Motivation #3:
"We want the picture and the feel-good story at the end of the week because of our work." Or: "Our church expects us to finish the project in one week."

We as Americans like getting jobs done. It makes us feel good about our work. There is nothing wrong with this, but is it the best? Many host organizations and ministries know this and work to give the short-term mission team a project they can finish in one week:

build a house, paint a wall, build a fence, etc. If our motivation is to get a project done in one week, more than likely we will get a project that can be accomplished in one week. But is this the best project we could have done for the community, church, or organization?

During a visit to a community that lives on the old Tijuana dump, I was having a conversation with the director who helps resource the people in the community. As we drove down the bumpy dirt road through the community, commenting on the different houses that had been built by Americans, we both came to the same realization. Though the wooden homes that were constructed by the American groups were good, they weren't the best that could be done for these families. In Mexico, most people who have the means build concrete block houses because they are more sturdy, last longer, and have better insulation. We realized that one of the only reasons we build wood houses is because the American groups can construct them in one week.

Yes, having a wood house is better than a tarp house, but is it the best we can give them? In Mexico, block is cheaper but takes longer to build and is more technical. Building a concrete block house in one week is hard. Don't get me wrong, there is nothing wrong with giving a family a new wood house. But let's be real, why are we giving them a wood house when we could give them a stronger block house? If it's because we want to get it done in one week so that we can feel good about ourselves and validate our trip, then let's be honest about our motivations. It is easy to do what has always been done, but look around, notice what is normal in the community, ask questions, and see if there is a way that has been missed. We need to look to what is best in each situation, not what is most convenient or self-serving—and be honest with ourselves, our team, and our church about why and how we are doing what we are doing.

Is it OK with your group and the organization you are working with if you don't get a project done in one week? Are you willing to yield to a project that would be better for the family or organization if the project takes longer than the week you have to give and you have to leave the project unfinished? What if your church or team decided to take on a project that would outlast your one-week trip and the church and team chose to fund the rest of the project? Your funds could be used to hire local labor, providing jobs to other people and, in the long run, give a better gift than what you could do in just one week. What if your goal was to leave a legacy, not a mark?

Conscious Motivation #4: "We are going to humbly serve, doing what they need us to do."

"Do nothing out of selfish ambition or vain conceit. Rather, in humility value others above yourselves, not looking to your own interests but each of you to the interests of the others" (Philippians 2:3-4).

These verses are the hallmark of a great, service-minded short-term mission trip. When we go into our mission trips with great humility, removing our selfish ambition and doing what is asked of us, the trip has the greatest possibility of being a success for all involved. When we surrender our agenda to the agenda of the host community's leadership, the trip works. When groups work out of the posture of being available to do what is asked and needed and not asking or demanding for anything unreasonable, "doing nothing out of selfish ambition," amazing things can happen.

When we leave for our short-term mission trips, many of us go with the thought that we are going to serve those in need and do so with a humble spirit. But when we enter into a culture or a community that we don't fully understand, where we can see the poverty and how people live, it is hard to not all of a sudden take on a fix-it, messiah complex.

Unconscious Motivation #4:
"They can't do this without us."

I love movies about heroes. It's no mistake that Marvel and DC continue to make movies about our favorite superheroes. If you are like me, I want to be the hero who comes to the rescue and saves the day, sets things right, gets the accolades, and leaves feeling good about the work I have done. But when it comes to our short-term mission trips, the last thing a community, church, or organization needs is for us to be the hero.

Though our motivation is to serve humbly, it is easy to get caught up in the moment and begin to think that if we don't get this job done or if we don't share the Gospel, the church or the orphanage will fail and people will be lost for all of eternity. We tell ourselves "they need us." As a result, we take on a Messiah complex and begin to force our way through the project while running over the very people we went to serve. We become the experts on how a project should be done or how an indigenous church should do ministry. Rarely, if ever, does this go well.

What typically happens when we take on the Messiah complex is that that host community or church feels devalued and dehumanized. We begin to force our way, our agenda, onto them without a regard to the work they have already done, without respecting their expertise and their knowledge of the needs of the community. Often serving with humility means asking for the help and insights of the host community.

When you are on the job site, do you care more about the people you are working with or the job you are trying to get done? When you step onto the job site, do you allow the local host to lead you and do it the way they want the job done? Do you submit your will, understanding of construction, and know-how to their professional understanding of how the project should be done in their community? Do you remind yourself that you are not the hero, you are just the servant?

What if we entered our short-term mission trips with an attitude of humility like Christ—who came to serve and not to be served nor even take credit for what He did? How amazing would it be if, after the trip, the people we worked with felt honored, dignified, and loved for who they are, for their gifts, talents, and leadership? We know what it is like when we feel encouraged and loved by someone else. Let us find ways to humbly serve and not believe that we are the heroes of the story, but we are merely the sidekick or the extras on a movie set while the true hero, the host community, is being built up in the Kingdom of God.

Humbly Navigating Our Motives While on the Trip

Our primary motive, spoken and unspoken, should always be focused on those we are going to serve. We must submit our agenda, needs, and desires to the ministry or organization we are serving and realize it is not about us; it's about them—their needs, their plan, their way of doing things. That's our side of the reciprocal relationship.

As we go about our trip, let's continually ask, "Are my words and actions matching my desire to humbly serve others?" How much do we complain when the shower runs out of hot water? How much do we complain if our living conditions aren't to our standards back at home? Do we follow the rules that are asked of us by the hosting organization, ministry, or church? Do we truly submit to the leadership of the hosting organization, ministry, or church, or do we blaze our own trail with our own agenda?

In short, do our actions and words communicate that we are there to serve the hosting community? Do they say that we really do care about those we want to serve?

It is possible to serve with the wrong attitude, an attitude contrary to what Paul talks about in Philippians 2, an attitude of pridefulness, arrogance, and self-centeredness. People who serve with an arrogant attitude are the ones who try to tell the local church how they should do ministry; they go with the intent of receiving praise and recognition for their work; they serve with the belief that what they have to offer is more important than what anyone else has to offer. They go forcing their will, their expectations, and their agenda on the host community—all under the guise of service. If we approach our trips with this attitude, not only will we miss what God wants to teach us, we will do damage to the community we go to serve. It would have been better had they not gone.

But it is possible to go on a trip with the hopes of learning and growing in our relationship with Jesus and others while serving others humbly. When we go with an attitude of humility, we allow ourselves to be learners, not teachers. We allow ourselves to learn new ways of doing ministry and construction. We allow ourselves to see the world through other people's eyes. We allow ourselves to develop good relationships with those we go to serve. When we have the attitude of humility, we will open ourselves up to learn, receive, and be led into deeper parts of life and faith. The attitude of humility allows for a reciprocal relationship to develop, and those relationships can further refine us because they allow others to help clarify our motives and point out when we're focused on ourselves.

It is through these reciprocal relationships that trust is developed and we are better equipped to serve each other more effectively. When we set our agenda and our pride to the side, we can listen better to the true needs of the community, being aware of how we can offer our gifts, talents, and resources. When we are humble, we can learn from and grow from each other. It is through reciprocal relationships that we will be able to take the shackles and weights off each other that keep us from growing into all that God has created us to become. This is our ultimate goal.

A Radical Change of Heart

Before we move on from our motivations into more practical discussions of how to develop relationships, we need to pause. It's not enough to have the right motives on paper and to diligently act on them—anyone can do that, at least in theory. But as Christians, what we're doing is different, and we're called to act with the heart of Christ. If our conscious and unconscious motivations are pure, we can avoid doing damage to communities—but without seeking Christ's heart, we won't be able to bring glimpses of His fullness to the communities we're working in and we won't be able to receive the glimpses of Christ that those communities offer us.

As I entered into ministry, the popular phrase of the day was, "What Would Jesus Do?" Even though this phrase is rarely used now, I would suggest we still ask this question on our short-term mission trips. "What would Jesus do if He saw someone hungry?" or, "What would Jesus do if He saw someone who didn't have a home?" But what if we take it a step further: "How would I treat and value the other person if he or she were Jesus?"

Jesus talked about this in Matthew 25: "Then the King will say to those on his right, 'Come, you who are blessed by my Father; take your inheritance, the kingdom prepared for you since the creation of the world. For I was hungry and you gave me something to eat, I was thirsty and you gave me something to drink, I was a stranger and you invited me in, I needed clothes and you clothed me, I was sick and you looked after me, I was in prison and you came to visit me'" (verses 34-36).

Jesus puts Himself as the one who is hungry, thirsty, in prison, naked, and sick. Jesus challenges us to consider, "Whatever you did for the least of these you did it to me." If we think about it, this makes sense. Jesus was always on the underside of life. He lived His earthly life as one who was poor, homeless, and oppressed.

Jesus, who is God Himself, took on the condition of the marginalized of His day. Jesus was born into poverty. Not long after He was born, Jesus and His family had to flee in fear of their lives as King Herod sought to kill every child under the age of 2. Therefore Jesus' family became refugees in a foreign country. Jesus lived as a homeless man enduring an oppressive Roman government who sought to rule through force and intimidation. He ate with the outcast and marginalized of His day. Jesus fought against the oppressive religious system that took advantage of people. Ultimately Jesus endured an illegal trial and suffered capital punishment. Jesus not only identified with the marginalized—He was also one of them. Even more surprising is that when He was confronted by the rich, He never asked for things. Jesus always pursued a relationship with others. Jesus never allowed the barriers of wealth, race, religion, or location to affect His desire for relationship.

I see this desire echoed in people I've met around the world. My wife and I were visiting one of our partners in Ghana. They took us on a walk through a village where many of the children come from who attend their school. Houses in this community were made out of adobe from the dirt in front of their houses. The roofs were made out of palm branches. It was some of the poorest living conditions I have ever seen. We stopped to talk to a mom of one of the children who attended the school. Not long after, plastic chairs were brought out under a tree, and then bags of cold water were purchased from a local seller, and we were invited to sit, drink water, and visit. Not once did this mom ask for anything. We just talked under the shade of the tree. Yes, this mom was living in extreme poverty, and we offered her nothing, except our time, our ears, and our hearts. There are many barriers between her and us, but sitting under that tree that hot afternoon, the only barrier was our language, but we spoke the same language of love, hospitality, and relationship.

This is a picture of the motivation Christ calls us to: to be with each other, no matter the barriers that separate us. Jesus broke these barriers down for us. What would our short-term mission trip look like if we saw the face of Jesus in *every* person we interacted with? We would become the learner and the servant. Learners and servants don't have all the answers. Learners and servants put themselves under another's authority. Learners and servants listen to understand before trying to solve the problem. Learners and servants do what is asked without complaining, leaving their agenda at home.

What if we saw everyone we serve with as part of the same family, the family of God—each of us reflecting the face of Christ to each other, each having something to contribute, and each striving to become all that God has created us to become?

DJ's 2 Cents

Being self-aware is complicated, and very few people do it well. It is necessary to have an honest assessment of ourselves, our true talents, and what we are presenting to the rest of the world around us. In short-term missions, being self-aware helps us to work in a healthy fashion.

Nothing in this world is 100%. Although mission teams go into the field to preach the Gospel or meet a physical need, there are always underlying multilayered motivations. I recently saw a joking ad for a "short-term mission selfie stick" to get the "best possible photos of you with poor children for your social media feed." It was funny because it cuts so close to the truth. People go to serve, but they also go for the experience, the travel, for something else to add to their college application, to look good on social media, etc. People are complicated.

Having mixed motivations is normal, but we need to be aware of our different motivations and do our best to serve others and build relationships from as healthy a place and motivation as possible.

One of the many privileges of hosting hundreds of short-term mission teams over the years is being able to observe the differences in the groups. We've been able to see a wide range of aptitudes, attitudes, funding, skill sets, goals, and other details that set groups apart. Sometimes these things set them apart for good reasons, many times for bad.

Without a doubt, our favorite groups are the ones that understand the bigger picture. They come down focused on working on a project and doing a quality job, but they realize that the projects themselves are irrelevant. The construction projects, the home builds, and the painting projects are just tools to build relationships. They understand that we are all in this together and they (or we) do not have everything figured out. Humility goes a very long way in mission work.

I've seen groups come down with a wide range of attitudes, ideas, and goals. I've had more than a few groups put together a very full agenda, completely broken down in 15-minute increments. Sometimes the biggest barrier to missions is our own agenda. These Americans have type A personalities and want to "accomplish something." I joke with some groups, "If you can't put a picture on Facebook, it never happened."

I had one leader tell me a story. After they returned from what I felt was a fantastic relationship-building trip, several people in their church had the same question: "But what did you do?" A trip can be wildly successful just by building relationships and listening to the people you're there to serve. A trip does not have to involve completing a house, holding an outreach, or organizing a VBS. The American mindset sometimes says, "If we're not incredibly busy, we are not important." Remember that Jesus did some of His best work just sitting around the campfire listening to those around Him and spending time with them. We can learn a lot from Jesus' example of being present with the people around Him.

CHAPTER 6

Learning to Feast Together

Phil

I grew up in a small country church in Northwest Ohio. I always looked forward to church potluck dinners. Let me tell you: my church knew how to do potlucks. There were at least three Sunday school rooms full of food lined up on eight-foot tables. The potluck always had its staples. The classic green Jello mold with fruit and nuts inside, countless varieties of casseroles, several pastas, and crock pots full of yumminess. There was the salad table section, including my favorite, the seven-layer salad. You could always count on a KFC bucket of chicken from a family who either forgot or ran out of time. What made potlucks so great wasn't just the fact that there was so much food, but it was because everyone was invited to contribute to the meal. Everyone had a place, and everyone's contribution was different. The potlucks brought our church together. Everyone felt valued, and there was something for everyone. And we all enjoyed the bounty together.

A potluck is a great illustration of what it means to have a reciprocal relationship. Everyone has a place and something valuable to share. Everyone gives, everyone receives, and therefore everyone is honored in the process. Far too often short-term mission trips feel like a catered event rather than a potluck—an event catered by American groups for the community they're visiting.

But in missions, it's not our table or theirs. It's God's, and He invites us all to bring our best and enjoy together. God has laid out the table of what He is doing in the world. He is already at work where we serve. When we step into another community on our short-term mission trips, we're not catering the event and getting all the credit. Instead, we're guests who bring a dish to a dinner that we have been invited to by God. When we step into a community on our short-term mission trip, we need to trust that God has been active in this community long before we got there, and He will continue to work long after we leave. We also need to remember that God has the same goal for every human being: to have a relationship with Him and grow to become the people He created them to be.

This point was driven home to me by my friend Javier. We were walking down the dusty paths that criss-cross the hills of the dump—full of garbage. Old plastic bags, tires, and other sorts of trash in various stages of decomposing. Javier, his wife, and many children live in a small, one-bedroom house in the dump. As we were walking, Javier took a big deep breath (did I mention we were walking on a trash dump?), and as he exhaled he said, "I am blessed." I thought to myself, *Blessed? How can you be blessed? You live on a trash dump with your family in a small one-room house!*

Javier continued, "I am blessed because I get to serve my community." He serves at a church that is located in the valley of this old dump. Every day he serves hot breakfast to children in his community before they go to school. He also serves short-term mission groups like ours by taking them to his friends to pray for them. "I don't get paid for doing any of this service, but I am blessed."

Javier sees everything he has as a blessing to give to others—a dish he brings to the potluck to share fully. One day, after selling some art that he makes out of scraps he finds in the dump, he realized he had an extra $10 in his pocket. "God, why do I have an extra $10?" he prayed. I could think of plenty of things he could buy with it or save it for. Instead Javier told me, "Not long after I prayed, there was a knock at the door, and someone was in need of money to buy tortillas and clean water. I realized why I had the extra $10, so I gave it all to my neighbor who was in need."

That view of life—that God has blessed me with bounty to share with others, even when my life doesn't seem like it has enough—is far from how many of us live. But to participate in a potluck, each one of us gets to bring what we have joyfully, holding nothing back. When we see ourselves as a guest at the table of what God is already doing in the community we are serving, and when we take time to listen to the voices of those we are serving with, we will hear the voice of God in others.

Opening ourselves to hear God in others, humbling ourselves to see that in God's eyes we are all the same, no better or worse than anyone else, is one of the biggest barriers the American church faces, yet short-term missions can demolish that barrier almost immediately.

One of our Be2Live high school trips is to a small community just south of the San Diego/Tijuana border in Mexico. As you drive across the U.S./Mexico border, the change in scenery from San Diego into Tijuana is quite drastic and immediate. As you drive west along the Mexico side of the border, you can see the 18-foot-high barbed wire fence that separates our two countries. On a clear day you can see the skyline of San Diego to the north. As you look south, you can see the dirty, run-down buildings and houses of Tijuana—graffiti-filled walls and shacks built along steep ravines with garbage on the hillside. After making the crossing, one of the high school students offered this reflection: "Yes, there is a wall that separates our two countries, but the dirt on one side of the wall is the same as the dirt on the other side of the wall. The dirt is the same. Yes, there are huge differences between them and us, but there are also some similarities. We are all people, human beings." We are all created from the same dirt. We are all created in the image of God. We are all invited into a relationship with Jesus. We are all called by God to serve. We all stand equal before God at the foot of the cross.

So we are all guests at God's potluck, called to the same purpose, our feet planted on the same dirt. What do we do next? How do we put these beliefs into action to transform our short-term mission trips? In this chapter, I'd like to share my story of building a reciprocal partnership as a case study and provide some practical steps to help you build similar partnerships.

Forming a Partnership: My Story

As a child, I was inspired by missionaries' stories of putting their complete faith in God's calling on their lives. During my church's mission conference, I would sneak out of the children's church to hear the stories. It was one of these times, during late elementary, that I responded to the visiting missionary's challenge—I would go anywhere, to anyone, at any time. First, I went on short-term mission trips with my youth group to Spain. Those experiences changed me. While working at YFC I helped lead trips to various places within and outside of the United States. Fast forward to when my wife and I were starting the youth group of a new church plant in California—we began to dream about facilitating a short-term mission trip to Mexico. Most of the youth groups we knew would go, build a house, and leave, never returning to the same location, church, or family, similar to what we had done in the past. God gave us a different vision. I wanted to find a community or an orphanage where we could build a long-term relationship for the long haul.

Through acquaintances I heard about a small community just north of Ensenada, Mexico. My wife and I went on a scouting trip and visited several ministries in the area. We were impressed with the intentionality of the ministries and the partnerships they had with the local community. After seeking God's leading, listening and learning, we decided this was the community where we were to sink some roots. Our first trip was in 2006 with 19 high school students and 5 adults; we went again a few months later with families from my church. The following year we went back, staying at the same orphanage, and the trip size doubled. Each year the students returned for their third, fourth, fifth time and brought their friends. Not only had my wife and I begun developing a long-term relationship with the orphanage, local ministries, and community but so did the students and leaders. In 2010 my wife and I launched our non-profit Be2Live, in response to God's leading and a desire to be more intentional in supporting and developing partnerships in the Bay Area, Mexico, and Ghana.

The first few years we made many mistakes, from doing donuts with vans in the riverbed that runs through the community, to not respecting some of the rules that were asked of our group by the orphanage, to taking photos of people's poverty in a sort of poverty tourism way. Some things we really were not aware of, but mainly we were thinking selfishly and not considering the deeper needs of the community. It is embarrassing to admit that we saw ourselves more as the saviors of this community and the people we were doing projects for. We didn't consider what we were doing or how our presence in the community affected not only them, but our group and our perspective on serving. We were not aware of the cultural nuances that a group like ours brought to a community.

Yet we were committed to a long-term humble relationship, and through that we were able to navigate our mistakes, make corrections, and learn things we weren't aware of when we started. Because of this commitment to the relationship—we kept coming back, asking questions, and listening to feedback—ministries and organizations we were working with lovingly and slowly revealed to us how we could do our work better. And the crazy thing is, it also helped them evaluate what effective ministry and partnerships in their area looked like. What we learned came from just being present, listening, and having a desire to learn. Many times what we learned was the result of mistakes other groups were making. Our posture grew as learners and listeners. We stopped seeing ourselves as saviors, but as partners in life with those we met.

As we expanded our partnerships with other ministries, we were connected to a young ministry in the old Tijuana dump. Their purpose was to help resource the emergency needs of the people. One of the first things they invited us to do was walk around the community, dispensing basic supplies to the families and praying with them. We were led by locals from the community to their neighbors who had need. As we walked and talked, we began to get a better understanding of the community and their needs. When we first started going, people would greet us on the street but never ask for anything. Over time we noticed more people hollering to our group, "Hey come pray and visit me." As we stayed present, listened, asked questions, and observed over time, we decided with the leaders that walking through the neighborhood handing out food wasn't the most effective thing for our groups to do. There was little reciprocal relationships developing, as it was us, the American group, handing food to them, the Mexicans. It didn't feel right, and there was a change in the community as more groups came to visit over several years' time—they realized that in the summers you didn't have to go find work, as the Americans were coming. This broke our hearts, knowing that our good intentions had a hand in helping shape this mentality, without meaning to.

We found ways to support the ministry more behind the scenes as well as resource and support the local soup kitchens that were run by the locals so that they would have the bandwidth to keep going. We began to explore new and different ways we could more effectively serve the community together because we took time to ask questions, observe, and listen to the deeper needs. We took time to listen to the people's stories in the community of how God had changed their lives.

We allowed the people in the community and those we were serving with to form and teach us how we could serve most effectively. We allowed ourselves to be led into the deeper needs of the community, not to try and solve the problem, but to simply listen and discover where the people in Mexico led us to serve.

It wasn't long before we learned how powerful stories were with our group. One night we invited DJ to share his story. That night rocked our team. The discussions we had after were amazing. Later that week we invited another ministry partner to share their story of starting a no-cost daycare in the same community. The director's stories impacted our students' lives in ways we couldn't imagine. The husband, along with his brothers and sisters grew up at an orphanage, abandoned by their mother. His wife had graduated college and was on the fast track to living the American dream when God got a hold of her heart while serving for a weekend at an orphanage in Mexico. She gave up her pursuit of the American dream and moved to Mexico. She eventually met her husband and a few years later opened a no-cost daycare to keep children off the streets and out of orphanages. Their story showed our team what is possible when you surrender your life to God's calling.

We come offering grunt labor to help further each ministry's vision and mission to help and reach their community more effectively and they offer their stories, their faith, their perspective that is life-changing. Through their stories and relationships we are able to better and more effectively serve each other and further the Kingdom of God.

As a result, we've been able to develop a reciprocal relationship that would've been impossible if we went to different ministries and locations every year.

Consumeristic Transactional Relationships

It's worth pausing to consider why so many churches and ministries go to different short-term mission locations each year. Like many of the challenges we've discussed with short-term missions, it's because of the consumer-driven, transactional nature of American Christianity.

We attend a church as long as it serves our needs, wants, and desires. We consciously or subconsciously rate the worship experience. We critique the pastor's sermon. Let's face it—most people choose a church based on what it can do for us. As long as the church meets the needs and expectations of the churchgoer (consumer), they will continue to go and possibly donate (transaction) to the church. There is no meaningful relationship, just meeting our needs of hunger and paying for what we experienced. The "church" works to maintain a customer through trendy programs, relevant messages, and a worship experience people will enjoy. It is strictly a consumeristic transactional relationship. Not what church or ministry is about.

Of course, it is important for us to find a place to belong where our spiritual needs are met, where good sound Biblical teaching is being taught. But when it reaches a level of a consumeristic relationship, it is an issue. We need to remind ourselves that church is not just for us; it is about the relationships we have with people at the church. It is about deepening our relationship with Jesus through studying Scripture and worshiping Him.

When we go on our short-term mission trips, we can carry the consumeristic transactional relationship mentality with us. Do we choose our location because of the relationships we have and can develop? Or do we choose a location based on going to new and exciting locations every year? One year we can go to the Dominican Republic and build houses. The next year we can go to Appalachia and repair houses that have been falling apart. Then the following year travel to Guatemala and perform skits in the park and hand out Bibles. We can do all of these "good" things. But with little to no relationship between those going and those ministering there long-term, is it the best we can do?

This model of going to different locations every year communicates to our students and ministry teams that missions and ministry mean short-term, transactional, consumeristic relationships that benefit me, the consumer. If we are bouncing around from one location to another, we are going on these trips solely for our benefit under the appearance of wanting to serve and love others. I know this sounds harsh, but why do we continue to bounce from one location to another every year? Who is the short-term mission trip really intended to help? If we believe that effective ministry in our own communities happens as the result of genuine long-term relationships, then we need to be consistent in our ministry and carry this forward into our short-term mission trips.

Growing Deeper in Relationship

It is human nature not to reveal weakness, needs, or hurts. We don't like people knowing what we really need because we are afraid of vulnerability and rejection. We don't reveal these needs unless we know the other person is safe, committed to the relationship, and actually cares about us. Ministries and organizations are the same; they don't want to reveal the deeper needs when they first meet us. They aren't sure if we can be trusted or if we are just there for the week, only to leave and never hear from us again. Trust only comes through relationships. If we care for those we are serving, we will go slow, build relationships, listen, wait for their leadership, and accept the task they put before us.

Many times the deeper needs of the community will take more than just a week to understand and help remedy. Though we are not able to do much in one week to remedy the deeper issues, we can at least be aware of them and find ways to come alongside the ministry throughout the year, whether that is through providing resources or prayer.

There are places where part of the deeper issues of the community are the short-term mission groups themselves who come to the community to serve. The long-term committed relationship provides honest discussions about the negative and positive effects our teams have in the community. We won't know this until we build these relationships and ask good questions. These conversations will not happen if we only come once and then go somewhere else the next year. Good and effective relationships take a long time to develop, and we must persevere and be patient.

We had been visiting a ministry and community where some of the poorest of the poor lived. The ministry invited us to bring boxes of food to visit some of the people in the community, providing food and prayer. We would divide into teams and be led by members who lived in the community and knew the people who were in need. We would walk through the community of pallet and plywood houses that were draped with tarps for roofs, delivering food and praying for families. This was a great experience for our group, but something felt off. For us, we didn't feel right that the "haves" were giving the "have nots" something. The experience felt more like poverty tourism than actually helping. It did not feel dignifying to the people we visited. So we stopped going for a while until we figured out how to do it differently. We had grown to love the ministry and the people we met from the community, but we wanted to find a way that we could serve in a more dignifying and honoring way. We sat down with the director of the ministry and shared our concerns and we came up with a different plan. Through our relationship, we began to find better ways to serve the community. Though not perfect, it moved in a more healthy direction. We began to do house maintenance projects, deliver clean water, serve meals at a local kitchen, and provide food for the *ministry* to hand out to the people in the community. Our funds pay for someone in the community to work with us, keep the kitchen open for people in the community after we leave, and keep a local water business going for another week. If it were not for the committed relationship with the community and the ministry, we would not have been able to find a way forward that was mutually benefiting.

Personally, when someone we have little to no contact with comes into our world and does something that offends us, we probably won't say much because we know that they are leaving soon. We wouldn't share our deeper issue with someone if we knew they were only here for a short time. Just like you and me, the hosting churches or communities we serve on our trips won't share their deeper needs either. Countless short-term mission groups have done things that have offended communities and ministries, yet the short-term mission teams don't even know it. The hosting community may not say anything because they know that if they can just endure the week, the group will go home.

Developing a Long-Term Reciprocal Relationship With a Community

This long-term committed relationship allows us to understand the deeper needs of the people in the community. Understanding these needs equips us to be more effective on our one or two-week mission trips. We will know how to better approach problems, ask better questions, and be able to listen better.

When we as leaders care deeply about the place we are serving and we commit to long-term relationships, the atmosphere of the trip changes for the better. Because we commit to the relationship, the people at the hosting organization become good friends and trust is earned. Students and participants care more about the people they are interacting with when they return throughout the year as well as between trips. Our team learns how to act within the community in a way that does not offend them. Because of the relationship, we come more humbly into the community. Our churches and the people we bring with us obtain a bigger vision of how they can be involved throughout the year and not just for one week.

So how do we develop these relationships?

Year-Round Communication

Communication is key to any relationship. But not just communication when it comes to the trip or logistics. Communication with the community you have committed to throughout the year is vital. Will we be there for them, connected to them, or care for and pray for them once the trip is over?

When I was a youth pastor at a local church, I wanted to set up a service opportunity for my youth group between Thanksgiving and Christmas. Of course, not being a good planner at the time, I was making these calls a few weeks in advance of the holidays. As I called different ministries and organizations in San Francisco and Oakland, I was unable to find any available time to volunteer. They were all booked. But I refused to stop looking. So I asked one church if there was any time available after Christmas. The person I was talking to said, "We don't have anyone signed up to volunteer the few weeks after Christmas. Everyone wants to serve between Thanksgiving and Christmas."

This is not meant to be a guilt trip but a realization that the people we served on our one-week trip are still there, many are still struggling, and ministries are still working hard to meet these needs after we leave. One of the thoughts that oftentimes gets verbalized on the last night of our trip is, "Well tomorrow it is back to the real world." This phrase irritates me. I know what they mean, but the orphanage they are serving *is* the real world for those orphans. The small wood house that was just built for a family *is* the real world for them, and tomorrow is another day with the same struggles. The family you gave food to and prayed for will still be there tomorrow, wondering when their next meal is coming. Tomorrow when we go home to our nice houses and hot showers, the people we leave behind will continue in the state they were in when we met them. They may have a house now, but many will continue to struggle to make ends meet. Indigenous churches, orphanages, and ministries that we served with on our trip will continue to work hard, many times on their own, meeting the needs of those they are working with every day.

Though we live in separate countries with different needs and live different lives, we should not forget the people we came in contact with while we served on our mission trip. We should find ways to continue to support the ministries, organizations, and people we met and worked with on our short-term mission trips.

Here are a few ideas:

- Commit to monthly check-ins with the people or ministries you served with, asking about their needs or any prayer requests.

- Find ways to serve and support them throughout the year, not just during the holiday season or when your trip is coming up.

- Ask them to pray for your church as well. Praying for each other is where the reciprocal nature of your relationship can grow and gain strength.

- When possible, invite them to share during your church service, either live or recorded. Keep the ministry in front of your church on a consistent basis.

When you report back to your church about your trip, talk about the people you met, their stories, how the church or ministry is doing, how your church can continue to support them as well as what you learned and how you grew. Give an update of your brothers and sisters on the mission field. Don't just talk about what the trip meant to you or what you did. Statistical outcomes (decisions made, Bibles passed out, etc.) are not as important as the relationships you built.

When we commit to a long-term relationship with those we are serving with on our short-term mission trips, a reciprocal relationship will develop. We will be able to more effectively serve each other, honor each other, and respect each other in God-fearing, God-honoring ways. Don't let the short-term mission trip be just a one-week summer fling. Make it one piece of a long-term relationship commitment.

Gauge Your Impact

If we are serious about developing a long-term relationship, we need to be aware of the negative impact we can have on the community we are serving, even unintended consequences. Have you heard of a carbon footprint? It is the measurement of how much carbon we individually and as a family emit into the atmosphere. It is the goal of

DJ Schuetze & Phil Steiner

many people to have a minimal to nonexistent carbon footprint to preserve the environment.

Similarly, we need to be aware of our "short-term mission trip footprint." How much of a negative impact is our group having on the organization? One of our goals should be to leave as little negative impact as possible on the community we serve so that we can preserve our relationship with them.

My wife and I have been married for almost twenty years. Like most marriages, there is a huge learning curve for everyone involved. When I was aware that Mindy was not doing OK or maybe I had done something that had hurt her, I could tell by the expression on her face or how the atmosphere was different in the room when she entered. Being the caring, loving husband, I would ask her, "Are you OK? Are we OK?" She would look at me with slight disgust on her face and say, "Everything is fine." In my mind I thought, "Well I asked, and she said she was fine, so everything must be OK." And I would go back to watching college football. Mindy wanted me to ask at least three times to show that I really cared. But I never knew this. I thought I was doing the loving thing by at least asking once.

We as short-term mission trip participants must pursue the host with our questions. Not to be overbearing or annoying, but to develop a better, more trusting relationship with the host.

It is good for the trip leader to check in with the host leader throughout the week and ask questions about the group's presence. Listen and don't settle for the first answer. If we want to have a healthy and developing relationship with the host community, then we need to pursue them.

Here are a few good questions:

- Is there anything we should be doing differently to make this a better experience for your community?

- Is there anything I need to be aware of in regard to our group or my leadership?

- Have we accidentally offended you, the church, or the community? If so, please let us know.

These simple humble questions asked throughout the week, and before or after the trip, will build trust with the host community. If you have offended someone, even if you did not mean to, you don't have a say in how the host leader feels. It is our responsibility, the offender, to seek forgiveness and make changes, even if it will affect our agenda for the trip. Remember our relationship is more important than our agenda. It is also good to ask the host community similar questions after the trip. We always want to be aware of our positive and negative impact.

Accepting the "No"

In our pursuit of a good, long-term reciprocal relationship, we need to be OK when the host community tells us "no." We may have great ideas of what we want to do at the orphanage, church, or in the community, but if the hosting organization says, "No, that won't work" or, "No, we don't need or want that," we as trip leaders need to be OK with their honest response.

"No, we don't want a VBS." Maybe it's because you will be the fifth VBS in the last five weeks!

"No, we don't want a concert and skit in the park." Maybe it is because the church has a different vision and understanding on how to reach their community.

"No, we don't need aquaponics (or insert special project)." Maybe it is because they could use those resources on the real needs of the organization.

We as leaders must be OK in accepting their "no" and work to discover where the true need is for the hosting organization. For those of you who host groups, please tell us "no" if it doesn't work into your vision, but then suggest what it is you are hoping that we would do. I know this comes at a risk, but in order for us all to pursue the type of reciprocal relationship we want, we need to be honest with each other.

As leaders, we should not be known as a high maintenance group. We should want to be one of those groups that when we ask to come back next year, the hosting organization is looking forward to our coming. Let us be groups that bring joy when we come by being aware of our footprint on the community and organization we go to serve.

If we have a desire to develop reciprocal relationships with the ministries we visit on our short-term mission trips, then it is essential that we commit to a long-term relationship. We cannot jump from one organization or country to another every year. Just like developing any long-term relationship, it takes time, work, struggle, and commitment. There will be successes and failures, clear communications, and at times miscommunication. There will be deep joys and confusion. But in my experience, you, your church, and the hosting organization will have a greater impact on everyone involved. Lives will be changed, visions will be furthered, impact will be greater, and God's Kingdom will be realized in the process. Go and do short-term missions and develop long-term reciprocal relationships.

DJ's 2 Cents

In any culture, relationships take time to build. If someone moves to a small town in the U.S., it might be years before they are not referred to as "the new guy." If a new pastor takes over a church, he needs to earn the trust of his new congregation, yet this does not happen in a week or two. If you're in a dating relationship, it would be odd to be completely transparent on a first date. It takes time to trust the other person, and allow our walls to come down.

When someone is coming into an area for only one or two weeks a year, it will take many trips to build trust and transparency. For relationships to build, commitment and understanding need to be shown. This doesn't happen in a week, no matter how great the week is or what our desires are. Relationships take time.

We instinctively know quality relationships take a great deal of time. For some reason, many people assume relationships will spontaneously happen when we show up in a small town in a foreign country, even though they are new to the people and to the culture. At our ministry in Mexico we refer to this as "hit and run" ministry. A group *might* do some good, but if we never see them again, the impact is temporary. Realize that to truly serve someone or somewhere, we need to listen, share, trust, and build relationships over time.

CHAPTER 7

Money in Missions

DJ

Money in missions is a huge topic. How we raise it, how we distribute it, and how to be responsible stewards of what limited monies exist. Jesus taught us that where our gold is, our heart will also be. Where do we use our resources and how? Since money is critical to making short-term trips happen, and because it's central to the power difference between host and visitor, how we view money, how we use it, and how we communicate about it can make or break the foundation of reciprocal relationships.

Few things generate more of an immediate emotional response than the topic of money. People have a natural, deep, emotional response to finances and the material wealth of this world. Jesus taught more on our response to money and worldly treasure than almost any other theme. This is important to God. The rich young ruler, the parable of the talents, the workers in the fields, and more. There's nothing inherently wrong with money, it's just dealing with it that's complicated. One of the most misquoted Bible verses is 1 Timothy 6:10 that money is the root of all evil. The verse actually says *love* of money is the root of all evil. Money matters, but what matters more is our response to it. It's a big topic, and we need to be mature and wise about it.

Money is a double-edged sword. Money handled with wisdom can change lives, communities, ministries, and the future of countries. Money handled poorly can destroy lives and communities. Whenever I meet with orphanage directors or mission leaders, the topic of fundraising always comes up. It's not why they're in the field, it's not their priority, but it's a reality of missions that it costs money. Money to care for children at risk, money to feed the needy, money to educate, etc.

Money changes relationships on many levels. If Bill Gates or Warren Buffett walked into a room of people they didn't know, everyone would know them right away, and tone would shift, comments would be made a little more carefully, reactions would change. If a family is a major donor at a church, even if no one but the head pastor knows, it still affects the relationship. The pastor might give special preference or he might not feel at ease keeping that family accountable. Unless the donor is very mature in his or her attitude, they might hold the donations over the pastor in subtle or not so subtle ways.

Most short-term mission teams are seen as financially wealthy, whether they see themselves as wealthy or not. Just by being able to afford to travel, you're already financially better off than most people in the world. Being seen as wealthy *will* change how you are received and treated, for good and bad. Be aware of this subtle shift that the perception of wealth brings into the mission relationship. "He who has the gold makes the rules" is truer than anyone wants to admit. That is why it's *so* important we realize we don't have the gold—it's all God's; we're simply entrusted with it to use it for His glory.

Several years ago we hosted a large group from the southeast U.S. at our orphanage in Baja, Mexico. We were happy to have them, but this group stood out for the wrong reasons. They flew 30 people across the U.S. to southern California, rented vans, and drove down to serve with us for five days. Most groups bring some type of funding to cover materials for projects while they're with us. This group brought $500 to use for projects and to bless our home. We appreciate any donation, but when I heard what they were doing the two days after they left us, it struck me as odd. The group of 30 traveled three hours north of us to finish out their mission trip by spending two days at Disneyland. There is nothing wrong with visiting Disneyland, but my guess is that those two days cost the group around $9,000 in tickets, lodging, and food. When the team was raising money to go and serve in Mexico, I wondered, were they transparent in letting donors know how much of the money would be spent on non-missional activity? Even if they spent their own money on the extras for the trip, is that the most productive use of their resources while on a mission trip? We did our best to make sure they had a great trip, but part of the joy of service is giving and blessing others. I think they may have missed out on experiencing some of that joy.

A few years ago my wife and I had the opportunity to serve with an orphanage in Ghana. We had some long conversations about the cost of this trip. My wife and I have over two decades of experience in running a very large orphanage. We felt we were bringing something of value to the home in Ghana and that we could make a substantial impact. We also knew that it would cost around $5,000 for the two of us to take this trip. We had to decide what would be the best use of that funds. Should we pay our way with the intention of blessing that home in the two weeks we're with them? Or should we just send them a check for $5,000? We had a responsibility to be good stewards of the funds we had available. In the end, we decided to go, and I'm glad we did. I believe the coaching we gave them helped in their fundraising that wound up generating ten times as much for that ministry as we spent to get there. We also decided to leave a financial donation to be used in any way they saw fit. I'm not sharing this to show how generous we are. I'm sharing this because I think it's a great policy to leave a substantial donation with whoever is hosting the short-term team. Call it "tithing your travel expenses" if you'd like.

We are called to be wise in our decisions and in our use of the resources we've been entrusted with. Our church, and God, wants us to make the most of the funds available to us. We need to seek healthy organizations wherever we're serving. Organizations that we partner with need to have a high level of accountability, a history of productive work, and a demonstration of responsible stewardship of the resources made available to them. We all need others to guide us and help us to be the best and most impactful we can be. These clear intentions, conversations, and actions about money allow us to remove barriers that make it difficult, if not impossible, to foster a truly reciprocal relationship.

Selecting Your Host: A Financial Perspective

To set the foundation for your relationship, work with a healthy on-the-ground organization in the country or area you feel led to serve. They know the people, they know the needs, and they know the impact and potential harm from visiting groups. A healthy hosting organization will also help you make the most of the funds you have available. Their financial health also allows them to interact more genuinely, with openness and reciprocity, not driven by deference or abundant need.

So how do you select a healthy organization? Never underestimate the power of prayerful, Spirit-led discernment, but there are some things common to most financially responsible organizations. It's a good idea to look for the following:

Is there financial transparency?

If the leaders of the organization are willing to share about their income streams and how they are managing funds, it's a good sign. People are more alike than we want to admit. A common red flag is how someone responds when the question of receipts or accountability comes up. I can't tell you how many times I've heard orphanage directors say, "What's the matter? You don't trust me?" It's not a question of trust; it's being good stewards of resources. In looking for financial transparency, like all areas of ministry, be conscious of cultural differences. Some cultures are much more private with this type of information. Finding the balance of pushing the cultural limits while looking for accountability needs to be subtle. You can work on building trust, but please know this takes time—more than you probably have on a short trip. I've found wrapping helpful questions in service back to them opens up some doors, and I truly do want to serve them. "Hey, I do a lot of fundraising—what have you found that works? Have you had better luck funding through individuals, churches, or other organizations?" These are honest questions, and you're not being manipulative if you honestly do want to learn and help them with their ministry.

How is the management living?

If the local leadership is living substantially above the people they are called to serve, this speaks to their heart. If an orphanage director in South Africa has a large house surrounded by sad rundown dorms, where are their priorities? If the local pastor you're serving in Mexico drives a brand-new SUV, and the people he's ministering to are walking or driving beat-up cars, what is that demonstrating? I'm not saying missionaries or pastors can't have nice things, but there needs to be a balance. I'm not saying all missionaries should live in destitute poverty, but as in any area, we need wisdom. If a pastor in the U.S. is driving a Mercedes when everyone in his church is driving a Chevy, it looks and feels wrong. Where are they putting their gold?

What are the organizational priorities?

Is the organization you want to work with serving *the* Kingdom or *their* kingdom? If a Christian is only worried about their own condition, their own comfort, their own well-being, that speaks to their maturity. The same thing is true of any missions organization. Any organization needs to be concerned with their community. If a church is only concerned with the people within their four walls, it's not a healthy situation. If an orphanage is only concerned with the children directly in their care, but not for children at risk in their area, it is not a healthy situation. Where is your potential host putting their efforts? Where are they spending their time? Where are they spending their resources? A great indication of a healthy on-the-ground organization is whether or not they have a healthy network with other missionaries, churches, and organizations working in their area. If you're going to serve at a facility and the project is painting the same wall over and over again, it's a problem. They are ignoring the needs of the community. An organization has a responsibility to be a good steward of all resources, not just financial ones. If you show up with a team of 20 people and you're doing busy work, the organization is missing an opportunity. Every town has needy families, schools in need of construction, and more; there are unlimited opportunities to serve. If you ask your host about visiting another organization and the leadership discourages it, or seems offended, that also shows which kingdom they are serving: their kingdom or God's Kingdom.

Is the ministry I'm partnering with just surviving?

Go to where the need is greatest, but think long and hard before you partner with a ministry in greatest need in that area. Our natural response is to help the neediest, but this doesn't, and shouldn't, apply to the neediest of ministries serving in an area. When you're selecting a church, you look at many criteria: theology, church culture, their approach to worship, their heart for missions. You would not choose to attend a church and support them with your tithes, your energy, and your time simply because it was the neediest, most destitute church in your area. The same standards should apply when we're choosing where we are going to spend our time, resources, and talents in the mission field. Let's put it another way: You are paying for a service. You are using your funds to have the mission host provide housing and maybe feed you. You are also entrusting them with your money to use it as effectively as possible for the Kingdom. If you were looking to spend money at a restaurant in your town to provide a meal for a small team from your church, which would you choose? Would you look for the restaurant that nobody goes to and is desperate for business to try to help them out? Or would you go to a restaurant with a line out the door because they know what they are doing and everyone has a great experience? You want to partner with people who are doing it right.

No organization is perfect, but if your receiving organization is in a constant state of financial need, has no established history of healthy fruit locally, and hides information from you, there might be a problem. You spending time and money for one week out of the year will not suddenly change them into responsible mature leaders who are good at what they do. You are only as good as the people you are partnering with in any endeavor. Choose wisely.

Wealth Is Relative

Just as it's unwise to financially partner with an organization that's not financially stable, it's unwise to give money to the neediest people. *Don't give money to the neediest? But that's the whole point of going!* I know one of your many goals is to help people in need, but it's important to do it wisely.

Too much money is just as bad as not enough. I know this phrase runs counter to everything about our American culture, where more money is always considered a good thing. But unless the people receiving the money are mature in their approach to it, and how to use, it will cause a great deal more harm than good.

Depending on where you are in the world, or where you are in life, different amounts of money can mean very different things. If you're in Southern California, $40 might mean dinner for two at a mid-range restaurant. If you're in an underdeveloped country in Africa, $40 might be a month's income. To hand somebody $100 in a developing country might be a huge blessing, or it might complicate their lives tremendously by causing jealousy among their family and friends, by giving them a false sense of security, maybe even by opening the door to temptations that would not be available to them otherwise. Money is power. Use it wisely, and give it to others in amounts and ways that help them to use it wisely also.

One example of a poor use of funds is handing money to children begging on the streets. I'm sure this opinion is going to offend some people, but it comes from years of experience. The need might be real, but many children in majority countries are trained to beg from a very young age and are frequently kept out of school so they can beg for loose change from tourists and mission teams. By giving them money directly, you might be helping their family today, but long-term you're encouraging the children to stay out of school and create a lifestyle of begging as opposed to working to move ahead. In running a large orphanage, it's common for us to take in children who have been on the streets, and many of them are experienced in the art of begging for loose change from visiting Americans. It takes a long time to teach them not to fall back on their old habits of begging. But over time, as their energies move from begging for quarters to schoolwork, athletic activities, and more, their whole demeanor and personality begin to change as their self-worth grows. They slowly move from the well-rehearsed, sad and pathetic faces to manipulate Americans, to faces of pride in what they are accomplishing.

In much of the world where short-term missions are common, or where there are large amounts of American tourists, many people and even organizations are incredibly talented in knowing how to pull at the heartstrings and manipulate the level of giving. We've all heard stories of organizations in Haiti or other majority nations misusing funds or just putting a show on for the visitors. We've all heard of, or been on, the "poverty tours." I know some orphanages intentionally keep their facilities rundown and depressing just for the purpose of manipulating American donors. There are some orphanages that have the children put on their frumpiest clothing if they know visitors are coming.

I was told about an organization in Guatemala that fully funded a school building three times; they would just change the dedication plaque on the building depending on which funding group was visiting. I know of one orphanage director in Mexico that always leaves a window broken because she knows many of the Americans she walks through the facility will slip her $50 to repair the window.

There are many well run and professional orphanages, but those few corrupt ones can spoil it for everyone else. Looks can be deceiving. Give wisely.

Relationships: A Wise Investment

We've talked at great length about not handing out money to the neediest. So what are we supposed to do? Partner with an on-the-ground missionary or organization that knows who and how to help. If you talk to anyone who runs a homeless shelter, the first thing they will tell you is "Please stop handing out money directly to people on the streets." Fill the need directly (hard to do) or give to a homeless shelter with a history of doing good work.

By choosing to work with someone who *knows* the area, the families, and the community, they can direct you to the people who can truly use the short-term help you are there to provide. They know the family with a father out of work; they know the family with the boy in the hospital; they know the school that is desperate for more desks; they know the student who needs just one more month of tuition to graduate. By working with a knowledgeable local, you can be led into having the most impact with the limited funds and time you have, wherever you are serving.

Please also consider using the local guide as a conduit if you're handing out funds because there is no real time for a relationship with the receiving individual. If the local missionary is working alongside the visitors, they know how to give and still respect the dignity of the person receiving the funds. It can be demeaning and awkward to have a group of Americans standing around while a poor family is handed cash; this is the exact wrong way to bless a family. As we covered earlier in this chapter, money changes relationships. Please give in a gracious, loving, sensitive way. Give, but give wisely.

After all these red flags, it's easy to wonder if investing in short-term missions is a good idea at all, but with a little thought, discernment, and communication, the money groups spend to travel and the money they invest during their trip can reap huge dividends.

Missions is a financial investment in the team.

Much has been written about short-term missions being a very poor stewardship of resources. Groups spend tens of thousands of dollars in travel and accommodations on a regular basis. Could the monies spent on travel be more effectively used by the organizations or missionaries hosting groups? Maybe, but it's the rare church or organization that will send this level of funding into the field without a team traveling out also. It's also rare to find an individual that would work as hard to raise money for a missions organization as they would to take their own mission trip. The experience is important.

We need to look at the intrinsic value of short-term missions. Short-term missions change the lives of the individuals on the mission teams. Maybe not 100% overnight, but the days and weeks spent in the field can and should become touchstones in people's lives.

Most people who go on short-term mission trips will not go into full-time missions, just like most people who walk into a church will not going to ministry full-time, but the church has tremendous value. One Sunday in a church probably won't fundamentally change someone. Attending church as an active member over the years can have a cumulative effect to change us and draw us closer to God. Working out once probably doesn't help us a whole lot, but an ongoing habit of regular exercise and nutrition changes us for the better. Short-term missions can be the equivalent of training for a spiritual triathlon. A week in Haiti or Mexico or China can have more of an impact on someone in their spiritual walk then a decade of Sunday mornings. This is money well spent. What is our spiritual growth worth?

Reciprocal Missions

The standard path for many people in the U.S. is to spend years and hundreds of thousands of dollars for a college degree. Few people wind up working in the field of their degree. A college degree is considered worth the expense because of the broadening effect it has on students and the doors it will open up in their lives. A degree is more than the classes. A degree is the cumulative experience of four years exposing yourself to new ideas and cultural experiences. Most people consider a college degree as money well spent. Short-term missions are much more than the small projects accomplished or the time spent sharing a VBS. A short-term mission trip is an education unto itself. People on a mission trip are exposed to new cultures, new ideas, and a new way to see the world. Travel begins to soften the American exceptionalism that most of us have.

It's a rare exception to find anyone in long-term missions who did not start out in short-term missions. It's that first step into the mission field that plants the seed, that shows needs out there in the world, and demonstrates to individuals the joy of serving and reaching others.

The changes can be hard to quantify, but the vast majority of people who experienced short-term missions in a healthy fashion are changed. They will refer back to their week in Africa or Haiti or Mexico as one of the touchstones of their lives. What is the value of that? How can you put a price on a changed life, a more fulfilling life, a more impactful life?

Missions fund missionaries and their work.

If a receiving organization or missionary is honest, a big reason they host groups is for the funding. This probably wasn't what they had in mind when they went into the mission field, but the reality is, hosting groups goes a long way to help fund missions organizations around the world. Groups can be a huge blessing, and at the same time they can be a tremendous amount of work. Hours spent in emails and phone calls preparing for the team, hours spent coordinating transportation and projects, hours spent sharing with the team once they arrive all take time away from whatever calling the missionary might have in that country. That's OK, as long as every-one is on the same page and the visiting team is appreciative and tries their best to bless the host and ministry as much as possible. Our hope is that however the group is serving, they are focused on honestly assisting the work of the in-country mission or missionary, and it's worth the time the host puts into preparing for the team. Please remember, your host needs to pay the bills also. Hosting groups helps missions stay open.

If the average group spends $20,000 getting to a location, but they wind up leaving a $2,000 or $3,000 donation to be used for the min-istry, that's money the ministry probably would not have received. There are also many other ways hosting short-term groups will help fund missions long-term. As in any organization, church, or retail business, the more people you have coming through your front door, the better you will do financially. If you own a clothing store, you know that a certain percentage of people who come in will buy something. If you own a restaurant, you know the average person might spend $30 to $40. If you pastor a church, you know a certain percentage of visitors will come back and a certain percentage of visitors will donate. The more people any organization receives, the better the income. Missions organizations are the same way. They know the more people who hear about and see the mission, the more people will choose to donate with ongoing support. Some people will really catch the vision, go home, and organize fundraisers or find other ways of supporting the work in the field. It's a numbers game with fundraising: if more people visit then more people will sponsor children, will support long-term, and will find creative ways to push the ministry along.

If the missionary is in a healthy place, it's not about the money. Our hope is that they are excited to see you either way and are look-ing forward to sharing their work and leading you into a life-changing missions experience. The money side of it is just part of the goal, but it is a reality in any ministry or organization. Everyone has to pay the bills.

Reciprocal Missions

Missions funding can transform communities.

In researching this chapter, I spent some time with several young adults who were raised in our orphanage and are now out on their own. I spent time asking them their opinions and feelings about the hundreds of short-term mission teams they've experienced. It turned into a long conversation, almost all of it positive. One of the things they discussed among themselves was the sheer economic impact short-term missions have had in our community.

We are a fairly small town, about 3,000 people. In our community there are two orphanages, a large free clinic, men's and women's rehab centers, and a free-of-charge daycare center. All of these ministries are supported by and through the short-term mission teams that come and visit our community. Many of the restaurants, mini-marts, hardware stores, and more are open today and are supported by the sheer volume of short-term teams that come to serve in our area. Collectively, more people are employed in our town, either directly or indirectly, through short-term missions than any other "industry" in our area. Is this the norm for most communities? No, absolutely not, but in areas with fewer teams visiting, the teams that do go can have an even greater impact. By locally buying food, building supplies, and whatever your team might need, you are providing jobs and pumping the local economy with fresh funds they would not see otherwise. There is a reason every city in America fights for convention business—people traveling to an area bring cash and can boost the local economy.

Some people put forth the argument that short-term mission teams can be detrimental to local economies by taking jobs local people could do. I fully understand that, but if the teams are managed correctly, and are partnering with solid on-the-ground ministries, the impact can and should be positive. We, and many other responsible organizations, take great pains to make sure any projects that groups work on are not taking away jobs from the local community. The projects can be geared to augment work opportunities through healthy partnerships.

We run a home-building ministry here in our town in Mexico. These are very nice homes, about 600 square feet with full electrical. These homes cost about $8,000 to build. The families receiving these homes are well screened and truly needy; it would take them years to build a home, yet we can bless them with one in about a week. At first glance, it's easy to say that the teams coming in are stealing construction jobs from the local community. Yet we know these home projects are adding jobs to the local community. The average family who receives these homes would never be able to hire the workers they would need to complete the construction. The construction would simply never happen. The family works alongside the visiting team, and we use some of the funding to hire other locals to work alongside, and this creates jobs that would not exist otherwise. We also work hard to purchase all of the building materials locally from community hardware stores—and $8,000 spent in a small local hardware store has a huge impact on their profits and their ability to provide jobs in the community. When managed correctly, short-term missions can have a profound, positive financial impact in small communities around the world. But any project has to be done in a correct, well-thought-out way.

Many years ago a small country in Africa had a thriving garment industry. Design, manufacturing, and distribution of clothing provided countless jobs. Over the course of a few years, well-meaning Americans started shipping in huge amounts of clothing to be given away. In time the clothing industry was wiped out. Stories like this are why it is so important to work with knowledgeable people on the ground who know their communities and how to guide your team. You can easily destroy an economy by giving too much or in the wrong way. Too often the mentality is "if we throw enough money at a problem, it will get better." Unless money is used in the right way, it can do just as much damage as an area winning the lottery. It might seem like a blessing, but ultimately it destroys.

There are plenty of example of people using the funding they have in a way that does no good or even causes harm. Last year a well-meaning group built a house in our area for a single mom with two children who had lost their home in an electrical fire. In that same fire the daughter was badly burned. As the group was leaving, one gentleman saw that the house was being powered by running a cord from the neighbor (not uncommon in much of the world). This very well-meaning man handed the lady over $1,000 to put in the electrical meter and have the house connected safely. That $1,000 was more money than she had ever seen in her life, and she did not have the experience to handle it well. Two weeks later she had a large new TV, a gaming system, and nothing left to wire the house correctly.

If teams are focused and wise in how they use the funds, a long-term positive impact is an attainable goal and can transform communities. When done right, micro-loans (small amounts, $25, $50, etc.) for small business start-ups can change lives. In our eyes these may seem like trivial amounts, but in much of the world it can be leveraged dramatically. For example, $25 worth of fruit resold at the local market might generate $35, and when reinvested in more fruit, it can slowly grow into a real business. Maybe it's a $50 loan for someone to purchase a sewing machine that they can use to produce sellable items. By setting it up as a loan, with small monthly payments expected, it's not a handout and preserves the receiver's pride and dignity. Partnering a micro-savings programs with solid, applicable financial advice can shift a person or family's future. Micro-savings might be just 25 cents a week, but over time, by encouraging this type of saving, it can give people a safety net.

Never Fully Fund a Ministry

I know this is going to puzzle or outright offend some people, but it's never a good idea to fully fund a ministry. You might think you're helping them, but you're creating an unhealthy dependence, and it's almost never healthy long-term for anybody involved. Again, putting relationships before money is the key to healthy, long-term impact.

If a wealthy family decided to fully fund a church in your town, the pastor or the board might be thrilled, but long-term it just doesn't work. Once the word gets out, no one else in the church would feel the need to give, leading them away from tithing as a way of honoring God. By not having it be a community effort, the church members would not emotionally "own" the church. With one family giving everything, would they try to sway church policy and would the pastor or deacons be willing to push back against the donor's influence? Eventually, if the funding family went broke, moved away, died, or for some reason stopped giving, what would happen to the church with no history of fundraising or giving? By the church being fully funded, it's hard to trust in God for provision.

I consulted with one orphanage where a single church from the U.S. funded everything. It was a nice system, and the home did OK for about 20 years. They charged almost nothing for groups to come and stay; they had no sponsorship program, no mailing list, no relationship with a donor base. They did have that one very nice check every month. That check was funding everything for the home. Over time, the relationship began to become a little strained and slowly fell apart. The church gave the home a full year's notice that they were pulling out (actually very generous). After the year was up, they backed out entirely. The orphanage and the home suffered greatly, as a year is not enough time to build a donor base. They eventually made it through, but it wasn't easy. The home had become way too dependent on the one big donor. They had no reason to work for more; they had no reason to trust in God.

If you sincerely want the ministry you're backing to grow and become healthy; you need to let them work to fund a large part of what they do. If it's a start-up, maybe fund them a lot more at first, but they need to know that you will be ramping down over time. They might need your coaching to learn how to raise money, but by coaching them to do it themselves, you are helping them more than you know. You are helping them to stand on their own. You are helping them to grow up as a ministry.

If you have a child, you would give them everything they need to survive when they are very young. Over the years, if you're a wise parent, you help that child to learn how to fend for themselves and grow into a self-sufficient adult. You would (I hope) never abandon your child, but you would want them to stand on their own. You don't want your child to be financially dependent on you forever; it's just unhealthy for everyone. You can be there for emergencies, maybe help with the down payment on a house, but if you're sending your 30-year-old adult child money to live on every month, you're doing it wrong.

Another reason to not fully fund a foreign ministry is a little more subtle. It doesn't matter how well everyone gets along in the beginning, if a U.S. organization is fully funding from a distance, if everyone isn't mature and aware of what might happen, it frequently goes sideways over time. The U.S. group tends to ask for more and more oversight. Oversight and accountability are normal and needed, but no one likes someone looking over their shoulder. Oversight can also sometimes be interpreted as being over-controlling: "We have the gold so we make the rules." The on-the-ground leader/missionary begins to bristle or resent the intrusion of the U.S. board over time. "I'm the one on the ground doing the work; why are they telling me what to do?" Also, no one likes to be 100% dependent on someone else; they begin to resent it and become bitter over time. Unless it's a very open, reciprocal, healthy relationship, it almost always ends badly.

No one church or funding agency should ever be more than about 20% of a foreign mission's ongoing budget. Fully funding is not good for the relationship, and it's not good for the long-term prospect of the mission. Fully fund them when they're starting out, fully fund special or emergency projects, but please help them stand on their own. It's better for everyone.

Trusting God; Acting Wisely

Money is a topic that will always bring a strong emotional response; that's OK—it's good to talk about it. What has been presented in this chapter is a very brief overview. We hope this helps to start some in-depth discussions with your church and your short-term mission team leaders. Members of your team will have strong opinions. You'll face disagreements, as we are all trying to be good stewards, growing in financial discernment. Pray and seek good advice from people who have gone before you, as well as people currently in the field. With the right preparation and research, you can make healthy impactful decisions with the funds you have available. These choice will build and preserve relationships with your hosts and their communities.

Phil's 2 Cents

Anytime money and missions or money and church are discussed, it can get messy and awkward. It's no mistake that Jesus talked more about money than he did about heaven and hell. Jesus knew that when money is involved in our relationships, ministry, and missions, it changes the dynamic. If we allow it, money can also destroy reciprocal relationships. Therefore it is important for us to be honest about the issue with each other.

One area that concerns me when it comes to churches or ministries who lead short-term mission trips is the money you bring for projects. If you are going on a short-term mission trip and you want to help with a construction project or do any type of work, please provide the needed funds for your work. Even if it's just $20 a person, something simple can go a long way. There have been many short-term mission trip groups who go to do a project but do not bring any money with them for the construction. If you do not intend on bringing money for the projects you will be doing, please don't go on the trip or find something else to do. Chances are high that the ministry you are going to serve is tight on funds for projects, as the majority of their money is going to support the ongoing ministry. Many of their resources are going directly to care for the people they are ministering to on a daily basis. Funding the ministry is already a difficult task, so please help by bringing your own funds to give toward the project.

CHAPTER 8

What to Ask Your Mission Host

DJ

I f reciprocal relationships are the linchpin of a successful mission trip, it's important to establish good communication with your host in order to build understanding and trust to prevent harm. Selecting and building a relationship with your in-country host is critical to your success with a short-term mission team. We've broken down the process into three areas:

1.   Learning about and selecting your host

2.   Building a relationship with your host

3.   Practical travel and logistics concerns

In all of this, please remember that you are seeking a healthy relationship. It's easy to fall into the consumer mentality of just finding a host to serve your group. Remember that you're seeking a partner, where it's a mutually beneficial relationship.

Learning About and Selecting Your Host

In 1953 Sir Edmund Hillary was just a man from New Zealand with an ambitious goal. He wanted to be the first to climb Mount Everest, the tallest mountain in the world. He was in great shape, he was bright, he had deep funding, but he didn't have what it would ultimately take to climb that mountain. He needed a guide. He needed someone who knew the area, the way around the obstacles, what to watch out for. He needed someone with on-the-ground experience with all the pitfalls and shortcuts. He found that guide in a local sherpa named Tenzing Norgay. Together, Sir Edmund and Tenzing accomplished what no one had done before—they climbed that mountain. What is your mission mountain? What kind of guide do you need to reach your mountaintop?

The importance of who leads you into missions, and the relationship you build with them, cannot be overstated. Without a guide, we stumble along, and we *might* find our way to whatever goal we're seeking, but the odds are against us. We need someone to shine the light on our path and show us what to do and, just as important, what to avoid. You are investing a tremendous amount of time, energy, and resources as the leader of the team, as the members of your team, and as a church. Finding the right host and guide is instrumental in helping you to be a good steward of everything invested in this mission trip. For lack of a better term, you need a "missions concierge" to help you make your time on the ground as productive as possible and help you reach your goals. Without a good on-the-ground host, it's impossible to know the true needs, the cultural details, and who to go to if something goes wrong. I know, thinking of your host as a "missions concierge" doesn't sound very reciprocal, but if the host's attitude is right, they are in this relationship to serve you as much as you want to serve them. It's just a give and take where everyone is trying to "out serve" the other and be selfless to one another.

A few years ago we were experiencing a busy spring break. We were hosting three large groups, and things were going pretty well. As is our goal, most of our groups were out serving in the community: working on food distribution, building a home for a poor family, etc. Late one morning, two vans pulled up and about 25 people got out. We weren't expecting this group, and they looked a little lost. They were staying at a nearby campground and their weeklong project was to build a house for a family they had met on a previous trip. It turns out, the day they arrived the family they were serving had someone in their extended family pass away, and the home building project needed to be put on hold. Suddenly the short-term team had a week in front of them with no plans. In talking to the leaders, I asked them, "So, who is your in-country host?" They looked at me like I was speaking a foreign language. "We just came down to serve. We figured with the home build we would be fine." Our team knew we needed to save this group. We gave them a tour, explained our ministry, and had them help serve lunch and do dishes. You could see the wave of relief wash over the leader just to be able to have their team do something, anything productive. Although they were staying offsite, they came back every day that week, and we were able to have productive projects for them; we even found some great projects for them in the surrounding community. At the end of the week, the leader pulled me aside and asked about checking dates for their next year's trip. They experienced firsthand how important it is to have someone on the ground where they wanted to serve.

As a tourist in a city you've never been to, you can wander around and you might stumble onto some cool things. You can get a guidebook, and that will lead you to certain areas you might be more interested in exploring. The best way to see a city is to find a local who really knows the town, its nuances, and can show you the back areas and notable spots that you would never find on your own. Please find your missionary local.

There are healthy churches, schools, orphanages, and missions organizations around the world interested in hosting your team. In my experience, there are a many more organizations that want to host you, but for the wrong motivations or from an unhealthy place.

Hosting organizations are like ministries anywhere—they are made up of people. Some great people, a few not so great people, and most in the fuzzy middle doing what they can. Consider the churches in your town. Chances are you visited and checked out a few churches before you decided where you would land. You attended a few services, maybe talked to some of the members, maybe even met with the pastor. You wanted to make sure you felt comfortable and that your priorities, beliefs, and goals were in line with the church you wanted to join. Can you be a Christian without joining a church? Absolutely. But being a member of a healthy church provides a healthy environment and provides the guidance and support we need to sustain and grow in our faith.

You might already have a great relationship with an organization, missionary, or pastor in whatever country you're traveling to. If you feel good about who you're serving alongside, fantastic—stay with them. Finding a stable, trustworthy ministry partner is rarer than you might think. Continue to work with them, back them, and continue to build that relationship. But if you're just starting out or want to look around at other options for short-term missions, here are a few things to think about.

The following are not in any order; it's not a complete list, nor are all qualities required to do a good job. These are just some things to consider. These can be indications of the attitude and mindset of your host organization.

Is the hosting ministry bearing fruit?

This can be hard to determine without building a relationship first, but it's a basic sign of good spiritual health. Are they just surviving, or are they growing? Are people drawn to their ministry, or do people leave and not come back? You will only be as effective and impactful as the ministry you're partnering with in your destination country. As your pastor and church should be guiding you into growth, keeping you accountable, and watching out for you, your missions host has all of those same responsibilities.

I'm not saying you shouldn't help the most needy where you are going; I'm saying you should be backing and helping the healthy ministries on the ground that are already serving the most needy in that area. There's a big difference between the two. You need a healthy ministry "middleman" who can direct your resources and efforts accurately to help you be as impactful as possible in the very short time you have. Honestly, your team probably won't make a significant impact on your own in a few days without a partner. If you're doing it all by yourself, or with a dysfunctional on-the-ground organization, you will not reach your goal. But if you're backing and building up a healthy established ministry, you will help them to continue the work long after you're gone, and you *can* have long-term impact.

Are they building the Kingdom or their kingdom?

As we said in the last chapter, if any ministry is healthy, it's working together with others in the community and seeking ways to reach beyond their walls to serve others. Does your host organization have good working relationships with other ministries in the area? Are they excited about sending groups out to serve in the community or with other ministries? Or do they have the groups they host work on the same projects over and over again, as long as it's their project? These sound like some fundamental issues but, as in a healthy church, a healthy missions hosting team is looking to build up anyone doing God's work, not just their own ministry. We should all be rooting for others' success in ministry. It's not a competition, and we do all serve the same boss. We need a Kingdom mentality and need to partner with like-minded people.

We can all get a little "turfy" sometimes; it's part of our human nature. If your pastor heard that you were attending a midweek Bible study in a different church and were getting a lot out of it, he might feel a little twinge of jealousy or insecurity. Even the best pastors are still human. We would hope a healthy pastor would be excited to hear about a member of his church growing in any way possible. If you were serving at an orphanage, for example, and asked about other orphanages in the area, your host might feel a little hurt or even a little threatened you might consider visiting another ministry. But if they were secure in their own calling and truly wanted this to be a great trip for you and as impactful as possible, they would be open to you visiting other ministries. I'm not saying this is a make or break point, but it is something to consider.

Do they have good "customer service" and/or hospitality?

I know this sounds contradictory to the idea that we shouldn't have a consumer mentality, but it's more about relational communication than salesmanship. A good indication of how they'll host you is how they respond to emails. You would be amazed at how few nonprofit or missions organizations have good email practices in place. Everyone gets busy, so if they don't answer your email within a few days, send them a reminder. If they still do not respond, are they that interested in hosting your team? If it seems like a battle getting information from them to help you along in your planning, odds are it will be the same when you're standing in front of them. A professionally run ministry is, sadly, kind of rare. Good, healthy, transparent communication is the basic building block of all relationships; in business, in ministry, in marriages, it always comes down to communication.

Check out the host's website or web presence. Is their social media or website up to date? Once again, people in ministries are usually swamped, but if they can't find time to keep their web presence up to date, will they have time for you? Check their website for a sense of service. If the website is only about the work they do and how to donate, it's OK, but it should also dedicate significant space to showing people how to visit, how to help, and what to expect. The website links are also an indication of whether or not they are working with other ministries. If all the links only lead back to themselves, they are *not* truly networking and working with other ministries in their area.

Reciprocal Missions

Once you get to your destination, are they ready for you?

Is your housing ready and presentable? Does the leader or member of the team welcome you, give you a tour, and make sure everything is OK? If you're working on a project, are the tools and materials in place and everything ready for you to get started? These are all indications of whether the host has a desire for you to have a productive trip or if they're just looking for your funding.

The question to ask yourself is: Why are they hosting us? The motivation to receive and host groups can have many different answers, and that's OK. Mixed motivations are the norm in any situation. Almost nothing is 100%. Do they want to help you in your vision to serve? Do they want you to partner with them in serving the people they are called to minister to? Do they want this trip to be life-changing and meaningful for your team? There is also the question that nobody talks about: Do they host groups only for the money and as a way to build their financial support? There is nothing wrong with having groups support the ministry—it's part of the deal and expected—but it shouldn't be the main priority when a group is being hosted. We all have mixed motivations, but with hosting organizations, as in church, the priorities are telling. This relationship you want to build goes both ways; examining expectations and motivations are key on both sides of the relationship.

Many organization tend to fall into the trap of seeing hosting groups as a necessary evil—something they dread, but they lower themselves to host as a way to fund the "real" ministry that they are working toward. Their priority is to use the groups for their own gain. They might host you, and your trip might be OK, but is that what you want? They should be hosting you because they are passionate about your experiences and leading you into the profound joy of service. We all have needs, but no healthy relationship should be self-serving, only looking out for your own best interest.

So keep an open, discerning mind as you feel out a new relationship. Like any relationship, nothing is perfect, but there are signs when it's the right connection. You make judgments like this all the time with friends, church involvement, dating, etc. You need to put the same effort into finding a great host and building a healthy reciprocal relationship with them.

Building a Relationship With Your Host

After you've selected a missionary or hosting organization to begin to build a relationship with, you need to take that first date. Whether it's your leadership team visiting ahead of your main team, an internet conference call, or even a phone call, you need to start building the relationship. Just like a first date, you can only learn about someone by asking questions: What are your hopes? What are your fears? What are your goals? Below are a few jumping off points to think about as you begin to build that relationship.

What keeps you up at night?

The phrasing of this is nuanced; it's subtly different than, "What do you worry about?" Several years ago I was meeting with some missionaries from a small country in Africa. The leaders of my team and I were seeking to dig below the surface and really get to know this very special couple living to rescue orphans. When I asked, "What do you worry about?" The gentleman from Kenya responded with polite phrasings and platitudes about him not worrying at all but only trusting in the Lord. This didn't really help us. I'm not saying we shouldn't trust in the Lord—I trust in the Lord, but that doesn't mean I don't have concerns about things now and then. It doesn't mean I don't bump up against challenges in ministry. I was trying to dig deeper and hear about his challenges and the attacks he fights in his day-to-day ministry. For some reason, when we reshaped the question to, "What keeps you up at night?" He really opened up. He shared the financial struggles, the struggles of corruption in the government, and his need for better staff and better staff training. This opened the door to us helping with staff training and led to some great discussions on choosing and maintaining staff in an orphanage. We couldn't help with the corrupt government, but we could let them know that we understand from our own experiences.

We were able to let them know that they weren't alone in their struggles. The simple question, "What keeps you up at night?" led to a great afternoon of sharing from both parties as we opened up and connected on a much deeper level.

This is what ministry is all about—connecting at a deeper level and experiencing that reciprocal relationship. As we shared what keeps *us* up at night, he was able to see that although we came from the other side of the world, we all had the same struggles. It was a profound afternoon of bonding and encouragement. That afternoon was the high-point of the trip.

I know personally, when someone asks, "What do you need and how can we help?" I frequently don't know how to answer. If they ask, "What keeps you up at night?" I can always name a few things. One of the reasons to ask about the worries of a ministry is that it can open the door to your team helping where the need is greatest and in areas you might have never considered. Your team might not have the resources or skill set to solve all the problems for a ministry in another country, but you'd be surprised what you might hear and the ways your team might be able to help. Maybe this school you are going to serve needs some basic IT troubleshooting or help setting up a website. Maybe the orphanage you are partnering with needs someone to come in and cover basic auto maintenance: oil changes, tune-ups, etc. on their worn-out fleet. Maybe the church you're partnering with for a week is desperately in need of a good sound person to set up or improve their sound system.

Another reason to ask a ministry about what keeps them up at night is it demonstrates to them that you are looking for a partnership, not just a place to crash. By asking this question, it shows them that you are concerned about their priorities. "What keeps you up at night?" is a question that is just a little more intimate than asking about their worries; it brings up a visual of someone lying in their bed, staring at the ceiling with eyes wide open.

Communication, communication, communication. At this point in this book, I hope you're catching on that communication on every level is what makes healthy relationships, and this leads to healthy, productive missions trips.

What was the worst group you ever had?

Anyone who hosts or has led groups has a few stories in them. Some are hilarious, some are embarrassing, some are scary. We hope that you're not the kind of group a host dreads. (You are obviously not a problem group, you bought this book!) It's good to be self-aware and realize that you're representing not only your church, you're also representing God, your home country, and frequently the mission hosting you. Are you representing them well?

We've had groups take a shopping day, and a few of the teens come back with marijuana (not legal where we are). We've had groups shoot off fireworks late at night in an area with real fire danger. I once had noise from a group wake me from a dead sleep at 1:00 a.m., and when I got up to quiet them down I found the *leaders* having a loud marshmallow fight around the campfire. More than a few times the local police chief has called me complaining about a youth group driving like maniacs or doing donuts in a field with a rental van. These are extreme examples, but examples like this happen all too often.

The worst groups we host are the ones that just don't care. They are on a trip *only* for their own experience, and their actions show a lack of respect for what we do and for the community and culture they are claiming to serve. For them, although they say, "We're just here to serve," their actions demonstrate exactly why they are here. We are merely a place to hold their summer camp and drape it with the title of "short-term mission" so they can sell the idea to their church and get people to fund it.

Communication, communication, communication. By asking about your host's worst groups, you show a deeper interest in what they do, and you allow them to pull back the curtain and share the struggles they've had with groups in the past. By allowing them to communicate their worst group stories, you not only learn what to avoid doing, you also get to see a little more into the host's heart. It's all about the relationship.

What's the best group you've ever had?

For all the horrible groups who've done short-term missions, there are many more who've done great things and shown hearts and passion for the destination country that are truly amazing. Some groups just get it. They want to learn from the host teams, they want to grow, they bring a fresh enthusiasm and vision.

By asking about the ideal group that a hosting organization is looking for, it can give you great insight into how to shape your trip to help in the most impactful way and truly be a blessing to the mission, not a hindrance. Maybe the organization can host up to 50, but they feel the ideal team size is around 20. Maybe they will tell you they can use any amount you feel led to donate, but to be effective the project/outreach/goals will cost about $2,000. It might be something simple like asking that you rent a van instead to having the ministry carry the burden of coming to the airport for you. They might tell you their ideal group would come off-season—most groups come in the summer or spring break to accommodate students, but the host ministry might really need you in the fall. It might be harder to pull off, but if it's actually about service you might need to make a few sacrifices.

Asking your host about the best teams they've ever hosted can be invaluable in guiding your group. Depending on how they answer can give you a clearer indication of how groups have worked well in the past to facilitate healthy, impactful short-term missions. What's "best" can be quite objective. Your host might be impressed with the visiting teams that bring in solid construction skills; they might be looking for teams that provide education; your hosts may default to the standard answers, but I would encourage you to push further. "No, no, what is the *best* group you've ever had?" My guess is, if they are honest, what made the best teams had nothing to do with projects, funding, or their ability to share the Gospel. My guess is the best teams are the ones who have a genuine concern for the host, the host's vision, and are willing to back that vision in spite of any pre-conceived agendas the groups might have. They are there to serve. Mission work and hosting teams can be phenomenally stressful and challenging on a daily basis. Just like any relationship, missionaries and hosts are drawn to people who demonstrate Christ's love.

For us, groups that think outside the norm are our favorite. We have a lot of groups that do crafts, play soccer, maybe make a meal for our kids. We've seen more piñatas than anyone should see in a lifetime. There are tried and true ways to help. All these things are good, but sometimes a group knocks one out of the park. We had one small church approach us about trying something different. They came in and took over a large multi-purpose room and turned it into a day spa. They brought in artsy candles, calm music, comfortable chairs, wall hangings, and curtains for privacy. Now, you might be thinking: "Why does 5-year-old Jose from the orphanage need a day spa? That's just weird." This group had a different vision. They knew what it was like to care for others full-time, and they knew our staff needed a break. They came in with the goal of serving the care-givers in our home. They gave pedicures to our cooks who are on their feet all day and have been for years. They gave manicures to the ladies in the nursery who use their hands to change dozens of diapers every day. They gave back rubs to the playground staff who need to chase, pick up, and care for crowds of toddlers every day. To be honest, our staff was a little uncomfortable at first. They were not used to being cared for in this way. Once our staff understood what was going on, it turned into a profound event. It's not often you get to see the example of foot washing that Jesus gives us played out in such a tangible way. The day spa happened years ago, but it's still talked about by our staff. They didn't spend a lot of money, they didn't put up a building, but their servant hearts came through on a tremendous level.

What do you wish visiting groups knew?

More often than you would think, missionaries and host organizations are hesitant to be transparent and honest with short-term team leaders. It might be a fear of offending or scaring you off; it might be a cultural difference. I have found that in Hispanic cultures, in the name of being polite, it doesn't matter what you ask or present as an idea, you will almost never be told no. As a visiting group, it helps to be humbly transparent and actually tell your host, "It's OK to say no, I won't be offended. I want to do a good job, and you know more than I do." You need to open the door wide for honest communication or it may never happen.

I once had an orphanage director come to me and express frustration that the groups only brought toys and candy. What she needed was fresh fruit, food in general, and cleaning supplies. She was afraid of telling her groups this because she was sure she would offend them. They were bringing this gift, and she didn't want to offend them by telling them it wasn't helpful. I had to coach her and explained to her that the teams wanted to bless her orphanage in a way that would be impactful. I knew if she were honest with them, they would go out of their way to help her in her areas of greatest need. When she told the first group that she needed fresh fruit for the kids, they went crazy (in a good way). That same afternoon the group drove to town and fully stocked her kitchen. Communication, communication, communication. She was happier, the group was thrilled to meet a real need, the children had healthy food. Everybody won, including the local fruit vendor.

Once again, by asking the right questions, you demonstrate an honest and sincere interest in serving the missionary or host organization on the ground and not just running your agenda. By asking the right questions, and *really* listening, you build a healthy relationship.

Practical Travel and Logistics Concerns

The following is a list of details that you will want to have addressed soon after you start planning your trip. Please do not make any assumptions on these—always double check.

Note: it might be a good idea to check out your host's website, as it might cover many of the items listed. Your host or missionary organization wants to help you, and they might have already made all of this information available to you if you look for it.

Logistics may not feel like deep relationship-building information, but preventing hassles, meeting expectations, and respecting protocols shows you care. It preserves you and your host's energy to relate well and do impactful work.

Visa and vaccination details: Ask what is needed. These things often change and, depending on the country you're traveling to, it might take months to make sure everything's in order. Many countries have a 90-day wait on visas, and some vaccinations require weeks to get sorted out. We know some people are against any vaccinations, so this will rule out many destination countries, as it's the law in many areas of the world. They will not let you in without the correct vaccinations: malaria, yellow fever, etc.

Transportation details: When traveling, you'll most likely handle the airline travel to your destination, but ask about ground travel. Is your host picking you up at the airport? Are you using public transportation? Is a rental car or van recommended? Whenever possible, take this burden off the shoulders of your hosts. Also, before you book your flights, ask if there is a best time of day for you to arrive and if there is a recommended airline for that area.

Dress code: The accepted dress code can vary dramatically even in the same country—church clothes, work clothes, what to wear in public can be very different than what we're used to. Always ask your host what is most respectful, and default to wearing something a little more modest than you probably do normally. Sometimes the nuances of dress code might surprise you. In our area of Mexico almost anything you would wear to church in the U.S. is OK in our church, but if males are outside doing physical labor, it's disrespectful to take your shirt off. Yoga pants might be acceptable at home, but are not viewed as acceptable in most of the world. You are judged on appearance more than you probably realize. Please be respectful, and represent the church and your country well. Protecting their reputation and avoiding conflict are vital to relationship and impact.

Housing: Should you bring sleeping bags or bedding? What are the restroom or shower situations? How reliable or available are power and water? For most groups, the simple reality of no hot water might be a shock. It's good to have as much information as possible to prepare your group for what to expect. In much of the world hot water is a luxury, and consistent electricity is pretty rare. Depending on your group, you might want to ask about the access to Wi-Fi also. If Wi-Fi is really important to you, you might want to set up a temporary international contract with your cell carrier.

How are meals handled? Once again, every missionary or host organization handles feeding the groups differently. Will you need to provide all of your own meals? Is catering available through either the ministry or a local business? As you plan out your meals, please be respectful of the fact that few organizations outside the U.S. are used to dealing with the many food allergies that Americans seem to bring with them. Gluten-free, vegetarian, vegan, and nut allergies can all make feeding a group complicated. Depending on the individuals on your team, you might want to bring a good supply of snacks or protein bars to fill in for any meals they cannot partake in.

What are the daily expectations for my group? Everyone hosts short-term missions differently. You might be expected to participate in daily prayer meetings or church services at an orphanage; you or your team might be asked to share or teach. If it's a work project, do they expect you to work a few hours a day, or the entire day, on the project? Are there any supplies or preparations that your group should be organizing before you come down? Managing expectations and having realistic expectations will go a long way in helping your team and the host organization to have a much better trip for all those involved.

What is expected with funding? Money is one of the realities that no one feels comfortable talking about, but expectations need to be communicated. How much does the organization charge for housing, for meals, for transportation, and other items? You will probably also be expected to cover materials for any construction or maintenance projects you're performing. As we discussed in an earlier part of this book, it's a good practice to leave a healthy general donation for your host or organization whenever possible. Consider it tithing on all of the money you spent on traveling to get to the host country. Another financial question that's good to ask is what are the local tipping customs: Do you tip the cab or bus driver? Do you tip in a restaurant? The cultural nuances of tipping vary widely from country to country, and you can offend just as easily by overtipping as undertipping. Once again, nobody likes talking about money, but how we handle it is a big deal.

Is there anything near the mission or ministry that my team should check out? This isn't just about going to tourist areas; ask about historical or culturally significant areas your team should visit to learn more about the hosts and the host country. Asking this demonstrates a respect for the host area and the desire to build a reciprocal relationship. These side trips are also a great way to show your team that every country has history, things they're passionate about, and things that we as Americans can learn. One side note on these local excursions: Unless they offer to take you or seem excited to take you, please realize your host has seen all of these sites many times before with many groups. They probably have more things to do than act as your tour guide; please be respectful of their time.

Missions need to work in both directions, and communication is essential. The questions presented in this chapter are a starting point to building healthy long-term relationships with your host or host organization. By asking the right questions, you not only learn about your host and the country you're traveling to, but you also demonstrate an honest desire to learn from them. You demonstrate that you are not coming in as the "American who already knows everything." By showing respect, you open the door to a richer, fuller, more productive long-term relationship.

Phil's 2 Cents

Knowing what to ask your prospective host is important to make you feel comfortable about the place you are considering taking people on your trip. But a word of caution: When asking your host the questions DJ gave you, do not fall into the American consumer mindset, seeking to get all your needs met. Do not make your choice of location solely on what the host can offer your group. Remember we are seeking a reciprocal relationship where everyone involved can benefit, and the host organization is going out of their way to provide a great experience for your group. They may not be able to offer everything you want, but they may be offering everything you need. Some amazing ministries do not have the resources to provide the creature comforts you may want for your trip, but don't decide whether you go or not based on your creature comforts.

Every new demand (often this is shrouded as a "request") adds to their workload. Honestly, what do we really need for a week on a short-term mission trip? Food, clean water, shelter, electricity, and a toilet (flushing or not). Everything else outside of our basic needs on a short-term mission trip is a luxury. Chances are, our accommodations are better than most of the people we are serving in the community. When we make demands/requests that are outside the scope of what has been provided or outside the scope of our host's ministry, we add to the host's stress and workload, distracting them from the ministry that we came to help.

As a leader, we need to walk the line of being sure our groups "needs" are provided for, while at the same time cultivating a humble servant attitude that focuses the trip not on ourselves but on others. Remember the short-term mission trip is not to be judged on the amenities the host provides like a hotel or a restaurant. If both host and trip leader are working toward a reciprocal relationship, your group's needs will be met to the best of the host's ability. So your reaction to the accommodations should be one of humble gratitude, knowing that your hosts have done everything they can to provide for your team. How great is it that they have invited you into their home to experience their community for the week!

CHAPTER 9

If You Host
Short-term Missions

DJ

If you're in the field receiving short-term mission teams, this is for you. It'll contain everything you need to know to host teams productively to impact the community you serve, prevent frustrations, and build strong relationships along the way.

If you're participating on a mission trip, or sending a team, you might want to read this chapter to see what it takes to host you well. This "behind the curtain" view will help you see the other half of a strong short-term mission relationship.

Why Do We Host Groups?

People are messy, and hosting is a lot of work, but if we're going to grow and grow the work we do, we need others. Hosting visitors and groups is probably bigger and more complicated than you had anticipated when you went into to the missions field. Hosting groups can take up huge amounts of time and energy. *How* we host and lead groups matters tremendously: to them, to our ministry, and to God.

We host groups for a collection of mixed and varied reasons. To expand the ministry. To help fund and build facilities. As a fundraising tool. To minister to and educate the people coming to us. All of these are valid reasons, and they can all apply simultaneously. In many ways, it's not about the reason itself; it's the careful consideration that goes into it.

We need others to partner with us in our goals or we will never be as effective as we want to be. Partnerships are critical to any ministry, both locally where we're serving and with teams and individuals from other areas. None of us know everything, can do everything, or have all of the gifts needed in our work. By networking with visiting groups and individuals, we are made better and can accomplish so much more than we imagine. The teams we're hosting can also frequently lead to networks of people willing to support us in our work, now and for years to come.

It's natural when we're serving children in need, families at risk, a church plant, a refugee program, etc., to focus on the people in the area we are called to serve. We are here to become more like Jesus, serve others, and proclaim the Gospel. Remember that it doesn't stop with the people we are "called" to serve. We need to represent Christ to *anyone* who crosses into our lives, including visitors from the U.S. we might be dreading, and those we may see as cutting into "real" ministry time. In my experience, and in talking to many other missionaries who host groups, even the best of visiting teams tend to triple our workload. Hosting groups is a lot of work and not for the faint of heart —just like missions in general.

Everyone has needs, wants their lives spoken into, needs healing; everyone has been orphaned in some way. We need to realize that hosting and receiving groups is a powerful ministry unto itself. Yes, in theory they're here to serve us. Yes, they're here to partner with us and help our ministries along. Most teams come saying, "We just want to be a blessing and serve where needed." But the people coming are frequently deeply wounded, under trained, and seeking healing, even if they don't know it. We need to speak into their lives, minister to their needs, be open to listen to anybody we cross paths with. Christ did some of His best work by the side of a well, with people He met on the road. He always had an eye and an ear out for where He could minister. We need that same heart if we're going to host groups in a healthy way.

Attitude Matters

After 20+ years of hosting groups, we get notes and emails from people serving around the world who had their first mission trip with us. How will a week with you impact and change the lives of your visitors? We need to lead people into life-changing, mountain-top experiences. God will do the work on their hearts, but we have a responsibly to lead them there.

For many people short-term missions is the first time they're stepping out of the pews to experience service on a deeper level. This might be their first time walking closer to the footsteps of Jesus with His heart to serve. For most people, a short-term mission trip can be a point in their lives they will remember forever as a transformational event in their walk with God. We have this incredible privilege of holding their hands and guiding them as they step out in their faith.

It's a rare exception to find someone in full-time missions who did not start out on a short-term mission trip. These trips are what God uses to speak to individuals about a deeper call for their lives, including long-term missions. These trips open their minds and expand their panorama of what God might have in store for them. When hosting groups, we have a responsibility to show them all that missions means. Not everyone is called into full-time missions, but some are. Of all the people who have joined my long-term team, many staying for years at a time, almost every person found us by starting with a short-term trip here.

If you're serving God, you're serving your brothers and sisters: whatever income, whatever country, whatever status they might have. We are called to serve those around us. Accept them as they are, as Christ accepts us. Christ has unlimited profound grace for us, way more than we could ever deserve. People are messy—each one of us is broken in some area; each one of us stumbles, falls; frequently we do more damage than good. But God has wildly abundant love for His children. He cheers at our feeble efforts, as a parent cheers when their toddler takes their first steps.

In hosting short-term missions, we need to be realistic: almost no one who partners with us for a week has the level of experience that we bring to the table. Our hope is that they come with enthusiasm, humility, and the right attitude. All too often, in their excitement and enthusiasm, they make more than a few messes. Puppies have excitement and enthusiasm, but we all know part of having a puppy is cleaning up the messes they leave, then lovingly training them to do better next time. Very few people going into short-term missions are housebroken. Let's lay out the newspaper.

Hosting 101

hos·pi·tal·i·ty (noun) 1. the friendly and generous reception and entertainment of guests, visitors, or strangers.

The gift of hospitality is real, and not everyone is gifted in this area. If you're going to host groups well, you'll need to learn hospitality or you'll need to find someone on your team with this vision. A person's experience with your ministry has a huge ripple effect. Are they going to leave excited about missions or turned off? Are they going to leave excited about your ministry? Will they leave wanting to share with others the powerful work that is going on? Or are they going to leave warning others to look for other places to serve? The first impressions and experiences they have with your ministry, odds are, will be the only impression and experience they have. You have one shot to make this work. Here's how.

1. Extend the open door.

Unless people know you host groups and are welcome to them, they won't come. I know this sounds obvious, but how are you getting the word out that you want groups to come?

Is your website clear that you want groups and have the ability to host? Does it have an appropriate level of details: costs involved, needs to fill, opportunities to serve, size of group you can host, etc.? Are you posting on Facebook or other social media, letting others know the positive impact groups have had on your work? Are you asking groups you've had in the past to help you spread the word about the work you do and your willingness to partner with others? Don't assume people know anything; share more than you think you need to, and then share again.

One frequently overlooked item: Take a long, honest look at your organization's email etiquette. Are you answering emails in a timely fashion? Are your emails well written, grammatically correct, and professional? For almost everyone, other than your website your first email to someone is the first impression of your ministry. If it takes you days to respond, what kind of impression is that giving them? How you respond clearly tells them that you are a professionally run organization that appreciates the help, or one that just doesn't care. I can't tell you how many groups wind up serving with our organization after they email many different ministries and we are the only one who responds.

A person will decide on a church in the first 5 minutes—ease of parking, did someone greet them, did the church feel welcoming? First impressions matter. We had completely ignored our website for a long time, and it was quite dated. I kept telling myself it was OK until someone told me "your ministry is much better than your site." I realized people were passing judgment on the whole ministry from our webpage. Once we redid our site, we started getting a much greater response and people contacting us just because our website was so cool.

Always be evaluating what impression your ministry is giving.

2. Evaluate the group's skills, goals, and agendas.

Jesus knew early on that His team wasn't ready for everything. When the apostles were starting out, Jesus knew the best they could handle was a simple "come and follow me." It took three years of training, mistakes, and corrections to get to the point where the apostles could "take up their cross." Proper evaluation of your visiting team is critical. This comes from a depth of communication from both you and the leaders you're working with. What are their expectations? What are their goals for their team? Where else have they served?

Not all groups are great at construction; not all groups are great at sharing the Gospel; very few groups are as mature as they should be. We need to meet them where they are and coach them along. At our organization we actually send an extensive survey to better plan and prepare for groups. Better information always makes for a better experience for all involved.

Everyone has different goals, expectations, and preconceived ideas of what a mission trip is. If you can help educate your group before they arrive, great, but not every group knows that they don't know everything. By asking the right questions, you can help them discover for themselves many of the questions they should be asking.

Some groups wants to get physically dirty. They expect to pour concrete, put up a building, drill a well. Do they have the skills and funding to complete quality projects in the short time they're with you? Will they need extensive supervision from your team? Some groups are much more relational. They want to do Vacation Bible Schools, community outreach, share the Gospel. Are they mature and realistic in their expectations? Are they culturally sensitive? Are they aware of the maturity level and true needs of the people they'll be ministering to, or are they running with their own assumptions? You get the idea. You need to know as much as possible about the traveling group to lead them in the right direction.

We don't have to cater to every group's whim, but we can lovingly lead them into the areas they have a desire to serve and where their gifts are best utilized. We also have a responsibility to lovingly lead them away from damaging or destroying any of the work we've tried so hard to accomplish. Almost all of Paul's writings to the early church were about guiding them into maturity and lovingly correcting them. The church as a whole has a long and rich history of screwing up. None of this is new. We need to be Paul to the groups, encouraging them and coaching them in the right directions.

Once you know what the team's goals and skills are, it's much easier to effectively utilize them for the Kingdom. They will only be with you a short time, so you need to leverage whatever skills and resources they are offering. They will have a better, richer experience, and your ministry will be better off.

While interviewing the leaders and evaluating any potential group, you might find out things you aren't thrilled with. It's pretty easy to pick out the groups that have a higher level of maturity versus the groups that only want to look good on Facebook and check "missions" off their to-do list. If there are some groups you might not want to work with, we'll cover saying no a little further on. But sometimes with weak groups we can have the greatest impact—you never know how God will move. These can be Solomon-like decisions, but with some experience and a lot of prayer, you will build relationships with the right groups at the right time.

3. Create realistic expectations and plans.

Before a group comes down, it's important to create grounded expectations. A group of 10 people landing in your town is not going to convert half the population, but their example of serving as Jesus may change a life or two. They're not going to transform a church, but they can encourage, serve, and partner with those on the ground. They're not going to end homelessness, but they can help build a house for a family. They may not return home with encyclopedic knowledge of missions, but they might learn about their place in the family of God.

Many groups tend to be overly ambitious. I've seen groups pull off enormous projects in a short period of time, but that is the exception. It's good to share with an incoming group from your experiences in the past. "In our experiences, most groups cannot put up a full building in a week. But if your team can help with the framing or laying the foundation that would be great." Once again, communication is critical to the groups having an impactful and long-lasting experience.

Even expectations with regards to housing, food, and other details are important to clearly communicate. It's OK to tell the group that housing will be "roughing it with cold showers." As long as they know the conditions going in, it will go a lot smoother. Creating realistic expectations is critical in any relationship.

4. Help them get to you.

Once a team has a trip planned, it helps tremendously if you can guide them through the unknowns of travel to your area. They can do their own research, but you know the shortcuts and details firsthand. What's needed in the way of visas? Do they need vaccinations to visit the area? What is the appropriate dress code? Will there be Wi-Fi or cell service available? Are there safety issues? All of these are great bits of information to calm the nerves and get everybody ready. A heart of service flows to all areas of hospitality. SHOW them you want them to join you.

You might consider addressing the "fear factor." Many Americans have never been out of the country, some have never been out of their home state. There are a lot of false impressions of what travelling to foreign countries is like and what the risks and dangers are. Be honest with visitors about appropriate precautions, but they are probably much more fearful than they need to be. Unless you're serving in a war zone, most cities and areas around the world are actually safer than many cities in the U.S.

5. Tell them what to bring.

Few groups want to come empty-handed beyond funding. It's OK to express needs that they can fill. By sharing this information, you are serving them in their desire to help and you're allowing them to partner with you. Tell them you need printer ink, that you miss U.S.

peanut butter, or that your staff would kill for some dark chocolate. These niceties help in any relationship. Trust me on this, they will appreciate your honesty and feel great about helping in a real way. (And you might get some chocolate out of the deal!)

6. Help them plan an agenda while keeping them flexible.

American teams (I'm assuming you are hosting Americans) tend to be very type A. They want to be organized and have set goals and a set schedule. You know very well this isn't the norm in most mission situations. You can assist the teams a great deal by helping them put together a realistic schedule, allowing for the inevitable power outages, vehicle breakdowns, or other challenges that come up daily in the field. Coach them ahead of time that flexibility is critical to everyone's sanity. They need a schedule, but it needs to be more of a guide than a hard and fast layout of their time. A balance needs to be found between keeping everybody on schedule and being flexible to changing needs and circumstances.

Encourage the teams to spend time debriefing while they're with you. These can be some of the best times for the groups, as they hear from each other the perceptions and reactions from the day's experiences. Everyone sees things through different eyes. Depending on the leaders, you might even give them some topics to bring up from previous group discussions. By slowing down and focusing in the now, it helps groups take in the events they've experienced at a deeper level.

Plan for down time for the team. No one who joins you for a week is going to be as committed to your cause as you are. If you're like most missionaries, down time is fairly rare, and you've probably gone weeks without a real day off. The groups traveling to you probably expect to spend a day doing touristy type activities. There's nothing wrong with those as long as it's not the focus of the trip. A day of rest is biblical, and it will give you a needed break.

7. Be ready when they arrive.

If you were having guests in your home for a weekend, you would make the appropriate preparations and be ready for planned activities. You would have their housing clean and presentable, you would want them to be as comfortable as possible. Hosting groups is the same way. You need to be ready before they arrive to host them; they are staying in your home.

If they're working on a construction project, you need to have all of the materials and tools on-site when the group arrives. If there's any prep work that needs to be done before the project can start, it should be done before they arrive. Odds are the group traveled extensively to reach you and they have limited days with you. They really don't want to stand around while you find the brick and cement for the project they thought would be there.

If your group is doing community outreach, have the preparations been made? If they're doing a VBS, or a service in the community, has the prep work been done? In many cases their activities need to be promoted correctly for days or weeks before the group arrives. We need to prepare the field for the laborers.

If you're housing the teams and groups on-site, put some thought into the level and type of housing you're providing. Dorms or apartments for groups don't have to be palatial or hotel level, but they should be clean, presentable, and well-maintained. As long as the group knows they need to bring bedding and be prepared for cold showers, that should be fine. If all you can provide is an outhouse, that's OK, just let the group know they will be tent camping. Just make sure that outhouse is as nice as you can make it, and make sure it has toilet paper. Once again, hospitality needs to be learned and made a part of your ministry culture.

It's OK to charge for housing, and every ministry needs to decide how to do that. We do everything we can to keep the prices we charge low so people can come and serve. Some ministries see the housing as their source of income and charge as much as they can. I don't know if there is a right answer here, but defaulting to the attitude of a servant's heart is always the best way to go.

8. Show them, educate them, guide them.

The best way to educate people about your work is to share your passion. Passion and excitement are contagious. If you're willing to be transparent and share why you're passionate about the work, others will catch your enthusiasm and vision.

There is a saying that time equals love. Spend time with the group, even if it's floating through at meal times asking how they're doing. Spend an evening sharing how you got called into ministry, share what your vision is, what your challenges are. Share of yourself.

When a team arrives, you can't expect them to know the subtle details of what goes on; you need to lead and educate them. If a new employee was starting, you would spend time explaining responsibilities, culture, expectations, and what important part of the team they're playing. When a group arrives they are your coworkers for a short time, but it's still their first day on the job. How you receive them and introduce the work will set the tone for their whole visit.

You do need to find the balance between guiding and hand-holding. This comes from knowing the group, the leaders, and what they're capable of. This goes back to evaluating the visiting team. Just like raising a child, you need to allow them to stretch their skills, but be there to help them when they fall.

9. Lead them into impactful work, not just busy work.

Assuming the group knows why they are with you, once a group is on-site you need to again give them a basic orientation of what you're going to have them do and why. People will catch on pretty quickly if you're just having them do busy work to keep them out of your way. They'll paint the wall, or clear the weeds from behind the buildings. They might even smile about it, but if it feels like you're just giving them non-essential work, no one is going to feel good about it, including yourself. If you're having them perform tasks that might not seem important to them, you need to share with them why it's crucial in the bigger picture.

I once had a group digging trenches for eight hours in the hot sun, and they were thrilled. If I had just showed them the marked off area and gave them shovels, they would've been frustrated pretty quickly, but I shared with them the reason they were digging the trenches. They were helping put in footings for a new infant care facility that would be caring for abandoned babies. Their work suddenly went from "we're moving dirt in the hot sun" to "we are helping save lives." How you present what they're working on matters a great deal.

10. It's really OK if they serve somewhere else.

Are you working to build *your* kingdom or *God's* Kingdom? This can require some deep, uncomfortable soul-searching for many people to answer. If you have a team at your disposal with skills, resources, or vision that doesn't fit your current needs or direction, help them serve where they can have the greatest impact. This can be painfully hard for a lot of people. Sending a team to serve with a nearby ministry is like a pastor getting up and telling his congregation to go visit another church next Sunday. Unless you are secure in what you do and your place in the Kingdom, this can be an intimidating and terrifying prospect. But, if we're here to serve the Kingdom and those in our influence, it cannot be only about us and our work. Everything we do needs to be about His work and furthering the Kingdom. We need to remember, none of this is ours anyway.

It's healthy to network with other missions and other missionaries in your area in order to work together to utilize all resources for the greater good. If this means sending a well-funded, talented group to another missions organization, that's OK. It's counterintuitive, but in my experience, the majority of the times we've sent groups to serve at other ministries have been incredibly productive. Not only do the groups have a greater impact, they also tend to become even more loyal when they see you're about expanding the Kingdom and not just hoarding resources for your kingdom. Remember, God's rules are very different than the world's rules. We need to be servants of all.

11. Follow up, and let them know you appreciate all they've done.

Two of the most powerful words in English language are "thank you." Most of us do not spend enough time showing gratitude to the people in our lives. When your group arrives, thank them for coming. During their stay with you, thank them along the way. When they get home, make sure they receive another thank you, even if it's as simple as a post referencing them on social media. Yes, they should be coming, serving, and helping because they have been called by God, and that should be their reward. But we represent God, so it's important to say, "Well done, thank you for partnering with us." We need to be flowing with gratitude.

On more than a few occasions I've had directors of other organizations tell me that to save money and time they send all their thank you letters out at the end of the year. This does not work. It's never too late to send a thank you, but a timely thank you means a lot more and shows that their efforts were recognized and valued by you.

Showing gratitude is part of building healthy meaningful relationships—do it! It's also helpful to share project updates, ministry updates, and general information with teams who've served alongside you. Yes, they might send more funds, but it's also an act of service to the groups, showing them you want them to continue to pray and be excited about the ministry. A great follow-up along with saying thank you is to ask the group how they are doing post trip. Ask sincere questions about their experiences on the trip. Show interest in them. Relationships take work, but they are worth it.

The Messy Stuff

It's OK to say no to a group, before or during their visit. Many groups come in with their own preconceived ideas and agendas; this is fine as long as they mesh with the goals of the ministry you're serving. Sometimes these goals and agendas are questionable at best or can actually be harmful to the goals that have been laid out, and even good intentions need flexibility.

We once had a well-meaning group ask us about building some very large chicken coops bordering on a professional size operation. On the surface it sounded great—free eggs for the orphanage—but something in my gut said this was a mistake. As a staff we decided to move ahead with the project. This well-meaning group spent tens of thousands of dollars and several months setting this up. When they we're done we had around 500 chickens producing eggs. Once again, on the surface, this sounds great. With a few months of egg production under our belt we did the numbers. After paying for extra staffing, feed, utilities, and more, it was much cheaper and easier to simply go buy eggs. We wound up eating a lot of chicken over the next several months and eventually converted the chicken barns into something we could actually use. Ironically, we wound up remodeled the chicken barns and converting them into dorms for groups.

When someone comes to you with a project, evaluate if the need they are desiring to fill is real. You also need to decide whether you or someone on your team can provide sufficient follow-up and management. Projects tend to come in trends. Years ago everyone wanted to install computer labs; right now the project everyone is pushing is hydroponic gardens. Unless someone is staying behind or you have someone on staff with a vision to maintain computer labs and hydroponic gardens, they are wasted efforts and funding. Orphanages and schools around the world have computer labs that gather dust because no one has the IT knowledge or vision to keep them up. I've seen dozens of hydroponic gardens either gathering dust or torn down to use the materials for other projects. These projects can work and be a huge blessing, but only if you have someone on your staff with the vision and energy to see it through. Is it something you really want? If a group is healthy at all, they'll understand if you explain that the project they have doesn't fit your goals. If a ministry in your area can use it and it's a good fit, send the group elsewhere.

With evangelistic outreach it's even more important that we honestly evaluate projects brought to us. Unless the group or individuals are partnering with a healthy local ministry or church, it's *very* hard to have a real impact. Help the teams by guiding them into effective and meaningful efforts.

In my town in Mexico we're close to the U.S. border and tend to get a lot of groups into our area. It seems like we have a big outreach concert in our town at least once a month, and our town is not that big. I know big outreaches can be effective, but they've been overdone in our area. Now when a group comes to me with this agenda, I try to graciously lead them in other directions: build a house for a poor family, partner with a local church with a project, maybe (with the church's blessing) partner with worship or VBS for a local church. The bottom line is you are the local guide on the ground, and you need to be good stewards of the groups at your disposal. The groups you're hosting will have greater impact and everyone will be better off.

If a brother offends us, we have very clear biblical instructions: go to them and talk it out. If a group or ministry isn't working out, please be honest with the leadership. One of two things will happen: they will leave and not come back, or they will change. Either of these results are good for you. We had a group that was sending teams four times a year (and they were quite well-funded). Over time they developed a bit of an edge or pride to them, and they became harder to work with. I sat the leaders down, assuming they would leave after the meeting and never come back; I was ready for that. When I opened our conversation with, "We host a lot of groups, yet you're the only one we dread," it got very quiet. I still remember the look on their faces. After a two-hour meeting, they left receiving the input well and truly changed their behavior. They've actually increased the number of groups they send, and we have a much better relationship today.

I opened up that conversation with a harsh line of "we dread your group" because I wanted to be clear with them how serious the situation was, but the whole meeting was based from the perspective of, "How can we heal this relationship?" They could feel our hurt *and* our desire to make it better for everyone. Transparency and healthy communication are critical in any relationship.

Sometimes you need to decide who you are going to work with or not work with. Some ministries will work with anyone, some are a little more selective, some will only work within their own denomination. You need to decide for you. If you're doing medical work or construction, are you OK working with secular groups? Rotary clubs, medical schools, and others can be great sources of assistance and can bring fantastic skills to the table, but they also bring unique challenges. I've had to explain to people why culturally they can't set up a full bar for their team here in the orphanage. It can be challenging to explain cultural dress codes to groups that don't understand they are representing your ministry in the area. On the flip side of this, we see hosting secular service teams as fantastic outreach; we're here to minister to them and show them Christ in action. By opening our doors to the unchurched, it's led to some great conversations and many changed lives. Remember, we need to reflect Christ to everyone we encounter.

People are going to tell you how to run your ministry. Everybody has an opinion on something. After running an orphanage for quite a while, I know most people who walk onto our property are judging what we do, and they think they can do it better. Everyone thinks they are an authority on parenting and missions. People have told me over the years that since we are in a tourist area, we need to build tennis courts to train our kids how to be tennis pros in the future. I've been told we need to be walking our pigs daily because it makes them healthier. The list goes on and on of people judging what we do or bringing ideas to us that make no sense. I've learned the skill of smiling, nodding, maybe lovingly trying to explain why an idea won't work, and moving on with my life. I frequently need to remember the many times I've told God how He should do His job. The grace God shows to us we need to show to others.

People are going to over-promise. Visiting a foreign country on a mission trip tends to be a mountaintop experience for many people. While in country they are excited and ready to commit their all.

Reciprocal Missions

Someone gave me a piece of advice when I started that I still hold onto: "Smile, be polite to everyone, and expect 10%." People will commit to funding buildings, donating vehicles, redoing your website after they get back to the U.S. They mean it at the time, but once they're home for a few weeks and "real" life takes over, promises can sometimes fall by the wayside. Once again, we need to show God's abundant grace. We can encourage (pester), but ultimately people are going to do or give what they want to. How often have we over-promised to God and then backed off once the emotion was gone?

We have a saying here (not one we put on the website): "All groups bring joy; some when they arrive, some when they leave." With proper evaluation, planning, and hosting, you can move most groups into bringing joy when they arrive.

Hosting short-term missions is worthy and powerful work. Like anything, if it's done right, it's a lot of work and can bring huge challenges. But this work is changing lives and transforming the church. If you're going to host, please do so with your whole heart.

Phil's 2 Cents

The American church and short-term mission teams needs you. I know that hosting groups can be a ton of work, and for some, a necessary evil. But the short-term mission teams needs your stories of faith, understanding of life, and your depth of wisdom. The American church has become stale, comfortable and apathetic. Your encouragement to the short-term mission team can change lives and change churches. The fire that is in you can spark a flame in the lives of hundreds of others because of your faithfulness to God's calling in your life. God can use your voice and your story to call others into full time ministry.

For me, it was the missionaries and indigenous people I met on these trips that changed my life. Their stories of God's faithfulness revealed a God who is alive and active. Because of their stories, I began to wonder, "What can God do in my life?" I began to pursue God more intentionally and now I am serving Him full time because of people like you.

I have seen how the stories of the people we have met while serving have changed the students and adults lives we take on these trips. People who were far from Jesus have been drawn closer to Him because of the people we met and their willingness to love and share their stories with our team. If you are a missionary or host short-term mission teams, please do not underestimate what God can do through you to change lives. Even for the most difficult team, your words and actions allow God to speak through you. As someone who leads short-term mission teams, thank you for hosting us and sharing your stories and lives with us. You are transforming lives. Don't give up!

If You Lead
Short-Term Missions

Phil

When I was 12 years old, my family took me on my first white-water rafting trip on the Snake River in Wyoming. It had been raining steadily for the past four days, and the river was high and moving fast. With my heart beating hard, I climbed on the raft with my family and our guide. Before we got into the rapids, the guide in the boat taught us how to work together to help move the raft through the rapids. The guide would yell out, "All forward!" We would all paddle forward. Then he yelled, "All back!" and we would all paddle backward. Then he yelled, "Left side back, right side forward!" and as we paddled, the raft began turning in a circle. He also informed us of the dangers ahead and what to do if someone fell out of the boat. Finally, after his instructions we began down the river. It was an exhilarating ride of rushing down the rapids and experiencing the trip together with my friends and family in the raft. Everyone, including the guide, got wet. We learned from each other. We depended on each other. We learned about the

Snake River and the surrounding scenery. We pointed out different things we noticed along the way. The guide moved our raft around dangerous areas, yelling out commands. When we reached calm waters, he would point out different rock formations and share history about the area.

The River and God's Movement

Facilitating a short-term mission trip is very much like a white-water rafting trip. Our role as leaders of the trip is to guide the boat into the river of God, experiencing the trip with those on our team, pointing out where we see Jesus has already been at work before we arrived, listening to people's stories of what God is doing in their family, church, or ministry, and joining Him in what He is already doing. Just like a river that's been flowing and keeps flowing, God's at work in a community before we get there, and He'll continue to work after we're gone. It is our responsibility to be in tune with God so that we can guide our team into the river—then everyone can experience His work in ways we normally wouldn't experience had we stayed home, thus growing more into the people God has created us to become.

In this chapter, we will discuss how to lead a reciprocal short-term mission trip. Good leadership is essential to the success of a reciprocal mission trip. How you lead will speak volumes, not only to the team you are taking, but to the host community leaders. Your vision, the culture you create, and how you act will determine the success or failure of the trip. It is an awesome responsibility—don't take it lightly.

The first part of this chapter will discuss the ethos of a reciprocal mission trip, and the second part will be more of the nuts and bolts of the trip. Every short-term mission trip needs both in order to build the reciprocal relationships that will make it a success.

If you host teams, this information can give you insight into how to best support groups and facilitate a good experience for everyone.

THE ETHOS

Simply put, a reciprocal mission trip seeks to partner with and develop a long-term committed relationship with a local organization, church, or ministry that will last far beyond the trip itself. Reciprocal mission trips think of themselves second, submitting their agenda to the agenda and vision of what the organization, church, or ministry hopes to accomplish while you are serving there. A reciprocal mission trip seeks out relationship before seeking out projects or events or photo opportunities. A reciprocal relationship is aware and in tune with God's movement in the community being served and between the group and the host, seeking to join God in His work.

Be Present, Be Observant, Be Available

There are three postures that we ask each trip participant to practice while they are on their short-term mission trip. Being present, being observant, and being available are three disciplines that will allow us to be open to what God is revealing to us on the trip and with our host ministry and community. These disciplines, if practiced, will help us to pause, look around and notice the work of God in our lives, not only while on the trip but in everyday life.

Be present.

We typically live in one of four areas: the past with our regrets, failures, or glory days; the future with our worries, fears, and doubts; on our phones distracted from the world around us; with God, who is alive and active in this present moment. Being present with God in the everyday moments of our lives will allow our hearts and minds to see His activity, especially on a short-term mission trip. Be present with God, be present with other people on the team, be present with those you are serving within the community. If we are present with each other, we will hear the voice of God, we will witness His activity in the world around us, and we will experience Him in new and different ways.

On our student trips, we do not allow cell phones or any electronics. It is amazing what happens to students when we remove their cell phone from their lives, how present they are to the world around them and the conversations that they have with each other. After the initial shock, students have told us how much stress is alleviated as a result of not having a cell phone on them during the trip. We ask our adult leaders to limit the use of their cell phones as much as possible, understanding that they have family and jobs they may need to stay connected to while being gone.

Be observant.

When we're not present to the world around us, it is difficult to be observant of what God is doing around us and in us. It is easy to get busy in the work we are doing or be so set on our agenda that we miss out on what God is doing right in front of us. We challenge our teams to slow down and look around them. What do you notice? Who do you see? What's different than what you are used to at home? What is the same? Not only should we be observant of what is going on around us, but we should be observant of what is going on inside of us. What are we feeling? What are we hearing God communicate to us? What are our thoughts as we see the people we are serving?

As leaders, it is vital for us to be aware of the impact our group is having on those we are serving. It is easy to get caught up in the needs of our group without pausing and being observant of the impact it is having outside of our immediate group, positive or negative. Pull yourself out of the trip and try to get a 500-foot view of what it is your group is doing. What do the locals think? What do their expressions indicate? When we are observant of the impact our group is having, then we can make the necessary adjustments on the trip so that we can have a successful experience for everyone involved.

Recently I was told a story of a group of students who were discussing their time in Mexico. One of the leaders asked what they thought about all the garbage that was in the community. One of the students suggested that the people in the community just didn't care about the environment or how clean their community appeared. The adult then informed them that the community does not have a garbage system. There is not a garbage truck that comes consistently to take their trash away. In fact, if there were that opportunity, many of them would not be able to afford the weekly garbage pickup. It wasn't about whether they cared about the environment or their community, it was that they did not have access to this simple "luxury" many of us Americans have back at home. When we ask questions about our observations and challenge our assumptions, we will discover amazing truths that we didn't know before. As a leader, we need to challenge the observations and thoughts that are mentioned by our team and try to dig deeper into them, looking for the truth.

Be available.

So much happens on a short-term mission trip. For those of us who lead these trips, we need to be aware of what God is doing, be willing to flex our agenda to God's leading, and be available to what the hosting organization is asking us to do. This will require us changing our schedule or even (gulp) our teaching plan for the week. But if we want the most out of our trips, we must be available to God as well as to those we are working with on the trip. Remember this trip is not about us, our group, or our agenda. It should be about God's leading, His agenda, and the host community, their needs, their desires, and their plans. Let us be available to whatever it is God wants to do with our group.

These three disciplines will challenge us in all areas of our lives, making a trip into a holistic experience. A reciprocal relationship will grow because we will be present, observant, and available to those we are serving because our hearts, souls, and minds will be open to engaging the host community in deeper relational levels.

Everything we do on a trip has a purpose, while at the same time, we must be open and available to shift. We believe that everything we do on the trip is spiritual formation. There is not a separation between spiritual and physical. It is all spiritual, and God can work through all circumstances; therefore we must be ready and aware of when this happens. We provide a lot of space mentally, emotionally, and spiritually to allow people to work out their beliefs and ask hard and uncomfortable questions so that they can wrestle with what they are learning and being challenged by.

I share my teaching time with those who live and work in the community. I want my group to hear the stories of people who I consider heroes of faith. Their perspectives on God, the world, and ministry always challenge my western, Americanized view of God and faith. It has been through these host stories that people in my groups have made dramatic life changes. It is through these stories that they see a God who is alive and active and they want that in their lives. If we are serious about the spiritual formation of our team, then we need to be open to having different voices speak into their lives, especially those who have sacrificed their lives for the Kingdom of God.

A well-developed ethos that centers on following God and developing reciprocal relationships is critical, but if we do not have the details of the trip nailed down, it will frustrate the ethos of the trip and could ruin what God wants to do.

THE NUTS AND BOLTS

Reading DJ's insights in the last chapter will help you know what to ask your host about. No matter what phase of the process you're in—before, during, or after the trip—let them lead you. Seek their expertise and submit to their needs and goals. Beyond that, here are some key areas to consider as you plan.

BEFORE THE TRIP

As a leader, we need to be able to dance between seeing the details of the trip while at the same time see the overarching view—whether you're by nature a detail person or a big picture person. I am not naturally a detailed person. I miss the details so easily it's almost like I'm trying to ignore them, even though I am not. But I need to dig down, think, make lists, think through every aspect of the trip, and be sure every detail of the trip is taken care of before going, while on the trip, and after the trip. I also need to hold these details loosely. I need to be able to be present in the moment while at the same time two steps in front of everyone. It is an art, a dance that leaders need to learn if we are to be successful in developing meaningful trip experiences including reciprocal relationships.

Setting Up the Trip With the Host

If you are looking for prospective places to develop a reciprocal relationship, visit our website (reciprocalmissions.com). When you find a place where you want to invest, let the host know your intention that you are interested in developing a long-term relationship. This may very well change the conversation and lower defenses. As you bring up the details of your first trip, discuss food, lodging, transportation, and projects. The host will be able to give you all the information you need in regard to in-country needs for your group. If you can do it, go to the community, church, or organization you will be working with for a setup trip. On the setup trip, get to know the area and potential safety concerns. A big piece of being in reciprocal relationship is not needing your hand to be held in every little detail. No ministry has time for that. You don't want to be a burden; you want to be a help. The more you can educate yourself on the area and cultural norms, the better it will be. Of course, you should spend time with the ministry leaders. This will give you a better understanding of what to expect, especially regarding housing and the atmosphere of the area. Your host will also give you an idea of what kind of project your team is going to do and any necessary tools you need to bring. If you are going to need any building supplies, ask your host where to purchase them in the country and in the community you are serving. In a reciprocal relationship, we want to benefit the community as much as possible; simply purchasing from the local store would go a long way.

Safety

Safety must be our number one concern on any short-term mission trip. We must continually think about the safety of the people we are bringing on a trip, especially in another country where emergency medical attention is not easily found. Find out where the nearest hospital is located. You need to know how will you get the medical attention you need if something happens. What happens if there is an accident while traveling to or from your destination? All of these safety details must be worked out and communicated to your trip leaders before going. We are caring for people, someone else's loved ones. It is a responsibility we cannot take lightly. I'm not a safety freak, but as the leader of a short-term mission trip to another country, it is my responsibility to ensure the safety of everyone going. Along with the above questions, here are a few other things we need before the trip.

1. *Medical Form.* Do you have a complete medical form that includes every person's medical insurance, policy numbers, health needs, allergies, food allergies, or dietary needs? If someone has allergies or medical needs, we follow up with a phone call to be sure we understand the situation. You will need to know if anyone on your team has any dietary needs or food allergies. Some places you go on your trips can accommodate dietary needs, while other places cannot, due to limited food options. On our medical form, we also have a release of liability and a media release area so we can use pictures and videos of adults and minors for promotional reasons.

2. *Boundary Form.* It's common for participants on a trip, young or old, to occasionally do something that is destructive to themselves, others, or the property of the place we are staying. We have a boun-

daries form that we discuss in meetings and ask every person to sign before the trip—and with minors, their parent must sign too. I am not one to have a lot of rules, but we do have boundaries that we expect everyone to observe if they are to go on one of our trips. Here is our list:

- If a person is found in possession of any alcohol, drugs, drug paraphernalia, fireworks, or firearms it is a one-way ticket home; if they are students, parents are coming to get them.

- No one pairs off in each other's dorms. Guys are blue, girls are red, and we do not want any purple!

- Respect for all leaders, and no bullying of anyone.

- No vandalism or destruction of property.

- We reserve the right to search any luggage if we think a person has something that is unsafe or something they shouldn't have (see above list).

Violating these boundaries has consequences that we outline to everyone before the trip. No one likes being the "heavy" and enforcing the consequences, but if you do not follow through on discipline, you will lose credibility with parents of minors and you will lose the respect and trust of the participants. This is the last thing you want on a cross-cultural trip.

3. *International Medical Insurance.* Check with your church or organization to know if they provide international medical insurance for your group in case of an emergency. Some have insurance that covers participants, while others do not. We ask participants to secure international medical insurance or check to see if their current insurance covers international travel.

4. Vaccinations. Research to know if the country you are going to requires vaccinations. The host organization can provide insight on this too. The CDC has a list of needed vaccinations depending on what country you are going to visit. For example, Ghana requires that every person who is entering the country be vaccinated for yellow fever. On our trips to countries that do not require vaccinations, we still require an updated tetanus shot.

5. Travel Documents. International travel these days is getting more complicated, and countries are changing requirements almost monthly. Keep up with these changes before your trip. It is good to research the needed travel documents way in advance. There are companies that specialize in obtaining visas; you will need to pay a little more for their services, but it is worth it as they will know exactly what you need and when you will need to apply for them. If we are facilitating a student trip, we collect all of their important documents once they no longer need them.

The paperwork necessary for a short-term mission trip can be overwhelming, but it is required for the safety and well being of everyone involved. This is my least favorite part of the trip, but it needs to be done. If you are not good at these details, find someone who will help you do this work.

Pre-trip Meetings

Lastly, as you get these pre-trip details in order, you will need to communicate this to everyone who is going, plus the families of any student participants. This will take the form of emails and other written communication, but a pre-trip meeting or several is an imperative element of the trip. People go on trips for many different reasons and motivations. It is essential to get everyone on the same page during pre-trip meetings. If everyone who is going is not in the boat paddling together, they will cause frustration and disruption to everyone else. As the leader, it is our responsibility to do the work to get everyone in the boat moving in the same direction.

Reciprocal Missions

If students are participating, it is essential to host a well-informed parent meeting. Developing and maintaining trust with parents cannot be overstated. Make it your goal to give your parents and families as much information as possible. Parents want to know *how* you will bring their student home safely and what safety precautions you are taking while on the trip. Go over in detail the packing list, schedule, and expectations for the trip. Treat this meeting as importantly as you treat the pre-trip participant meeting to gain trust, respect, and support.

Here are my main topics for preparation:

1. Vision. This cannot be highlighted enough. Just as safety is weaved throughout the entirety of the trip, so our vision should be also. Why are we going? What do we hope the outcomes of the trip are for the community we are serving and our team? We hope that as a result of reading this book, your will have a reciprocal vision for your team and the people you are serving. Hammer home to your team that this trip is not about you, it is not about numbers, and it isn't about getting the job done. It is about being present, observant, and available to what God is doing and taking on the form of a humble servant. Yes, it will be uncomfortable. Yes, it may be hard. But we are going for the benefit of others, and it will be worth it.

2. Team Building. Team building is part of being present with each other on the trip. Spend time having your team get to know each other through different exercises and talking to each other through small groups. This is important, especially if you have participants who don't know each other well. The initial conversations, even though they may be shallow, will get your team familiar with each other so that you can discuss deeper things sooner on the trip. Relationships are central to your impact, and they begin within the team.

3. Cultural Awareness. Learn as much as you can about the country you are visiting before going. What are the cultural differences that your team needs to be aware of so that you do not offend anyone?

Ask the host about what you need to be aware of while in the country you are going. In Ghana using your left hand is considered offensive. In Brazil giving the OK sign is the same as flipping someone off. The last thing you want to do is to offend the people you are working with on your trip, damaging the chance of a reciprocal relationship. Also, as Americans, we can be pretty loud and rude and not even realize it (i.e. sarcasm doesn't always transfer to other cultures). As the leader of the trip, please be aware of your group's volume and how you are acting while in the community.

4. *Dress Code.* Along with cultural awareness is understanding appropriate dress. This is a big one. There are many things that may be culturally appropriate in the United States that are not appropriate or are offensive in other countries, such as yoga pants, bikinis, saggy jeans, short shorts, revealing mid-drifts, taking your shirt off to work, certain colored T-shirts, logos, and tattoos. We give participants a reminder and ask them to change if necessary, and if it continues to be an issue, we provide culturally appropriate clothing for them. (Usually once this happens, especially to students, they magically find more appropriate clothing in their bag.) This is another way that teams can easily honor or dishonor their hosts, and this affects relationships.

5. *Addressing Our Assumptions.* We should be aware of the religious and cultural context we are coming from, knowing that this will have an impact on how we view the people and the community we work with during the week. We won't be able to remove our contextual lenses completely, but we can at least begin to get a look through someone else's perspective on faith and life. Addressing our assumptions before the trip will help us get a better view and understanding of the country or city we are going. Later in this chapter we will discuss the importance of challenging our assumptions, but it is important to bring our assumptions to the surface during our pre-trip meetings. One of the criticisms of short-term missions is that we do not take the time to address our assumptions about people in the country we are going to serve, about poverty, and the different cul-

tural customs. If we can begin discussing our assumptions before going, it will be easier to address them while on the trip. There are two prompts I bring up that help get at our assumptions:

People from (insert country or city) are_____.

What comes to your mind when you think of (insert country or city)?

I ask everyone to write these down and then share them. It is amazing what people think about people in other countries and cities as well as their view of that country or city. Keep the sheets of paper that they wrote their answers on and bring them back up while on the trip to see if their assumptions were correct or not.

6. *Spiritual Formation.* Everything we do is spiritual formation: from the team building to the cultural awareness to addressing our assumptions. We need to allow God to speak to us through everything we do, not just the times we open our Bibles and talk about the Scripture we are reading. Yes, provide space for the focused spiritual elements—large group teaching and small groups, devotions for the trip, a verse for the trip, and more, but don't divide the spiritual from the physical, mental, or emotional. It is all formational if we allow ourselves to hear God in all of it. I would encourage you to talk with your team about the verses we shared in chapter 2, discuss the importance of what and why you are going on the trip, as well as what it means to have a reciprocal relationship with the people you are going to serve.

Leader Recruitment and Training

Recruiting leaders for your trip is an important element to the success of your trip. Even with adult-only trips, you need a few key point people who can assist with organization, accountability, and pertinent travel details. The last thing you need is to be concerned about how your leaders are acting and what they are saying. Good leaders can be hard to find. For student trips, we typically try to avoid having parents of the students on the trip, unless the son or daughter gives their parent permission to participate. The last thing we want is a helicopter parent who will hover over every step their student takes while on the trip. If you have a parent come, outline clear boundaries that they are not to parent their student, but to be a leader.

Once you have your team, it is essential to not only go over the logistics of the trip with your leaders but also share the ethos of the trip or what you want the trip to feel like for the team. Clearly communicate your vision and what you hope to accomplish. You will need a team of leaders pulling in the same direction you are pulling to make the trip a success.

DURING THE TRIP

For me, this is where the fun begins. You have done all the pre-work, the forms are collected, and everyone has their travel documents. Now how do we execute a successful trip?

Travel Groups

I know we all travel differently, but I wanted to give you an idea of what we do on our trips. When we travel by air, we will divide into travel groups. These travel groups begin at the airport. Each travel group will have one to two adults with a small group of students. I prearrange these groups so there is no confusion the day of the trip. Each travel group will check in together, go through security together, and walk to the gate together. We will collect every minor's travel documents after getting through security to make sure these remain safe until we need them again. Once at the gate the group can go get food, returning in time to board. When it is time to board, the leader of the travel group is responsible for making sure their group gets on the plane. These are also the same groups that will be in the vans as we travel.

Reciprocal Missions

Arrival

Once you arrive, meet your host, and have them welcome your team, be sure to work with the host to share any immediate information. Many times this will include house rules. We must pay attention to these rules, as we are guests in their house and therefore we should abide by their dress code, quiet hours, when meals are served, appropriate actions, etc. As the leader, revisit these rules throughout the week, especially if your group forgets.

Sometime during the first day on site, check in with the host leader about any changes to the projects or schedule. We have a term for this in Mexico—it's called Flexico Mexico. We need to be willing to flex and change if it helps the local organization we are working with on our trip.

Daily Host Check-Ins

An important element to developing a reciprocal relationship is to check in with the host on a consistent basis. Check in to be sure your group hasn't done anything wrong or hasn't offended anyone. Check in to see how the host is doing. Spend time building a relationship with the hosts, getting to know more about them while you are there.

Caring for Leaders

Your team leaders are the backbone of your trip. Other than safety, how you support, love, and care for your leaders will either make or break the trip. Find out what snacks or simple pleasures they enjoy. One year we had a leader who always put whip cream on her coffee. She was willing to give this up for the week. But on the first day of the trip, as our leaders were getting their coffee, we pulled out the whip cream for her. The expression on her face said it all, as she was shocked and grateful that we thought enough to bring something simple, communicating that we cared. Find simple ways to love your leaders through small acts of love, demonstrating gratefulness that they are on the trip with you.

Daily Leader Check-Ins

As the head leader, it is always important to check in with your other leaders, making sure they are doing OK and if there are any issues you need to be aware of each day. Share the schedule for the day, any changes to the day, and other details they need to be aware of that are coming up. Also check in to see how all student participants are doing; what do they hear the students discussing, the positives and the negatives? It is good to get a pulse on your group throughout the day.

On the Work Sites

If your group is doing a work project, spend time checking in with the participants, leaders, and local workers that are on site. Remember, communication is key to developing a long-term reciprocal relationship. You want to be responsible and respectful of how your group uses their time, work tools, and work opportunities. Often workers in other countries are surprised by how poorly American teams care for their tools. Be mindful of how you treat the local tools you are given to use. Work hard, but spend time getting to know the people around you. I have had many great conversations with students while working alongside them, talking about their family, school, life, and stresses back home. Again, use this as spiritual formation.

Challenging Assumptions

As leaders, it is our responsibility to help our team work through their assumptions. Many people who go on short-term mission trips with wrong assumptions return home finding ways to confirm these false assumptions because we don't take the time to process and challenge them. As a facilitator of these trips, it is our responsibility to challenge our group's assumptions about the people we are working with on our trips. Here are some ideas on how to challenge assumptions:

Reciprocal Missions

1. Team Meetings. During our evening teaching times on the trip, we typically do a quick up-front game to get us laughing, and if we have someone who can play music, we sing a few songs together. Then we debrief our day, remembering our three disciplines of being present, observant, and available. During this time people have the opportunity to share what they have noticed about their day, about God and about the people they are working with on the project. This can be a powerful time as people dare to share what they are learning. It is also a great opportunity to push back against any assumptions that might arise. Here is one that typically comes up that we need to address: "They are so happy, even though they have so little." I challenge this assumption by asking follow-up questions:

- Do we know what that person's home life is after we leave and they close the door behind them?

- Did we get a chance to talk to them to understand their life, their struggles, their home situation?

- Do we know these people well enough to understand if they are truly happy with what they have, or are we making an assumption based on a brief interaction with them?

I don't ask these questions to make people feel bad or guilty. I ask them out of love, wanting them to wrestle with things we may not have thought about before. I don't want them assuming things about other people that aren't true. I wouldn't want people to assume things about me that aren't true either.

Because of American exceptionalism, we believe that everyone wants to be like us or move to the United States. We assume that they want our way of life, our wealth, and our way of doing things. Not long ago I had a conversation with an older woman who lives in the old Tijuana dump. She had lived a few years in the United States, and currently her family lives there as well. As I was talking to her about her family and her time in the United States, she told me, "I want to go back and visit my family, but I don't want to live there. I didn't like it there. It was too much." Presently today, more Mexicans are moving to Mexico than they are moving to the United States, either legally or illegally.[9] I have conversations with second-generation students who miss their home back in Mexico or Latin America, and they do not like living in the United States.

One of the best ways to challenge people's assumptions is to simply ask questions about what people verbalize, ask about what they observe and feel. Don't settle for the first answer. Every night we debrief our day around the three disciplines. What did you hear today? What did you see, feel, think? Then ask follow-up questions. Dig deeper into why people think the way they are thinking. Partway through the trip, these meetings are a great time to pull out those papers we collected during the pre-trip meeting about our assumptions.

2. Invite local leaders to share. One of the best ways to work through our assumptions, as well as hear God from a different perspective than we are used to, is to invite a local leader, pastor, or community person to share with our team. It is my desire for our group to learn from these leaders and what God has taught them about life and faith. My agenda for the week and what I want our groups to learn is wrapped up in learning from the people we are serving. I don't understand why we would travel to another community and not ask the ministry leaders or members in that community to share their stories and perspective on life and God. We have so much to learn from people, especially from a non-Western and non-American Christianity. If we are to take a look around the world, we will see the church exploding in the non-Western World, especially Africa, Asia, and South America. I would suggest that if anyone knows how to "present the Gospel" and live a life of faith, it is the church in the majority world. We, the American church, have much to learn from churches and ministries in the places we go to serve. Inviting local people to share develops reciprocal relationships be-

---

[9] http://www.pewhispanic.org/2015/11/19/more-mexicans-leaving-than-coming-to-the-u-s/

cause it shows we value their voice and their perspective in our lives. This can go a long way to growing our relationship with each other.

3. *Find educational opportunities.* Take time to educate your team on the different issues and history of the area in which you are serving. It will provide a bigger picture and understanding of what your group and the ministry or organization you are working with are doing in the community and why they are doing it. We live in a time where the world seems to be in chaos, and there are major issues taking place everywhere. Many, if not all, of our short-term mission trips are to locations that are experiencing injustices such as cyclical poverty, abandoned children, slavery, lack of women's rights, oppression, racism, and the list can go on. We need to help people navigate and critically think about these issues. The world is in need of Christ-loving, peacemaking, justice-seeking individuals. These trips are an opportunity to help develop these Christ-like characteristics.

In Mexico we have opportunities to discuss child abandonment, cyclical poverty, orphan care, and immigration. In the inner city, there is an opportunity to discuss systemic racism, poverty, and oppression. Whether we realize it or not, the places we go on our short-term mission trips are experiencing some injustice that has perpetuated the need we are trying to fill. Justice asks the question, "Why?" Why are there orphans? Why are generations of families in poverty? Why do women not have the same rights as men? Why are people of color segregated into the projects of our inner cities? Why is there still slavery? Why are there children begging for money? Things don't just happen. There is a history, a story of how things got to be how they are today.

It can be hard to know what injustices are happening in the area or understand the underlying issues. Therefore, to get below the surface, we need to find the leaders that are pushing back the tides of injustice. Ask them to come and share about their work, the injustices in the community, and what they are doing to combat it. When we hear stories of how people are being treated, it humanizes the issue.

When we humanize the issue, the injustice now has a person, a name, and a story attached to it. This changes everything!

On our trips to Ghana, we visit the Cape Coast slave castle, a holding place for slaves during the trans-Atlantic slave trade, and learn about the history of slavery and how Ghana is connected to the United States through this atrocity. In Mexico, we visit the border wall that separates the United States and Mexico, discussing immigration, deportation, and the many lives that are affected by this human-made barrier. We invite people to share their stories of the work they are doing to help alleviate injustices in our world, whether that be the director of an orphanage or people on the front lines, freeing children from slavery.

Communicating & Debriefing With Parents

For student trips: Parents are the most influential person in a student's life, and therefore it is imperative for us to communicate to parents as much as possible about students' experiences. Since students do not have their cell phones, we set up a daily blog on our website. We inform parents with as much detail as possible what the group did that day from work projects, the people we met, as well as stories about the ministries we worked with while on the trip. We try to post at least one picture of their student every day on our social media pages as well. Then on the last night of the trip, we post a list of questions that parents can ask their students when they get home. Inform the parents about what reentry may be like for their student as parents will be excited to see them and have a lot of questions. It is my goal that students will debrief the trip with their parents in a meaningful way. When they verbalize their experience, it will sink from their head into their heart. Plus, I want parents bought into what we are doing so that we gain their trust for future trips and events we do with their students.

Reciprocal Missions

Preparing for Reentry

Your group has spent the entire week immersed in a different country or city away from the normalities of life. They have been living a different pace and have had an intense experience while on the trip. It is essential to talk to your team about what it will be like when they return home. For us, our team of students have been in Mexico, without their cell phones, away from many of their friends, family, and technology. In the same day, these students will go from living at an orphanage where they have been working hard, getting dirty, to a nice clean home with a hot shower and good water pressure. Some of them cry when they get home, some do not quite know how to process the week and are quiet, while others will talk their parent's ears off until 2:00 in the morning. As the leader, it is important to bring up reentry and talk about it. I tell the students that they don't need to return every text message, Snapchat or Facebook post. Ease back into your home life gradually.

Leading a trip can be fun and frustrating. But take advantage of every opportunity to help your group grow and be formed by the Holy Spirit. Spend time with the local leaders, listening to their joys and struggles. Find areas where your church or organization can begin to invest in the ministry or community over the long haul. Finally, please go back, at least a few more times, and maintain connection throughout the year to develop a committed, long-term, reciprocal relationship.

AFTER THE TRIP

It is easy to let the one-week short-term mission trip be just that—a one week experience that we leave in the place we were serving. The time after the trip is key to a reciprocal relationship, solidifying the change in the lives of those who go and the connections to the community where you served. Don't let it be just a one-week trip, do something at home. Don't forget the people you met and what God is doing in the community where you served.

DJ Schuetze & Phil Steiner

Take Action at Home

Challenge your team to consider the following questions: What can you do to bring about meaningful change in your community, neighborhood, or family? Where can you tangibly demonstrate love at your school or at work? Who in your world needs a loving hand or an encouraging note? Where is God leading you in your life, career, or future? What can you do to take what you learned back at home? The last night of the short-term mission trip is not the end—it is the beginning to a different way of life, a new start with Jesus, a renewed energy for living into the life God has called you to live. The trip should be a catalyst for life change back at home. As the leader, your team is going to need you to remind them of this trip, the experience, and all they learned. Challenge them to do something with the experience.

We have had churches catch a bigger vision for their community back at home, beginning to reach out to churches in under-resourced parts of town and work together to help support these poor communities. We have had other people get involved with justice issues back home. One student, after hearing about a daycare in Mexico that was fighting an injustice of keeping children off the streets and families together, went to her local Chinese restaurant and asked for hundreds of takeout boxes. She decorated the sides of them with pictures and statistics of the needs in the community where the daycare was located. She then passed them out to friends and family members, asking them to put the takeout boxes on their dryers, and anytime they came across loose change, drop it into the Dryer Buddy. Over the course of the year, she raised well over $3,000.

One of the hardest parts of a short-term mission trip is to take what we learned and experienced and make it stick back at home. As I'm sure you are aware, about 4-6 weeks after returning, many participants return to their old habits, acting as if the trip never happened. But as the leader (and boat guide), I know it is my responsibility to continue the conversation, realizing that the mission trip is not the destination to get to but a moment in time on the long journey of life with Jesus.

Reciprocal Missions

Follow-Up Meetings

One of the best ways to maintain the impact of the trip is to continue to meet after the trip, remembering what happened, the things you learned, the commitments made, and how you are applying it to your life today. Weave what you learned from the experience into other aspects of your ministry. After an intensely shared experience, chances are your group has developed a deep trust with each other. This is a great opportunity to maintain and even deepen the impact of the trip. Another way to continue to maintain the experience is to find places to serve as a team in the community.

Remembering the People You Met

Remember our goal is to develop long-term reciprocal relationships with those we are serving during our one-week mission trip. The best way we can develop this relationship is by maintaining contact with them throughout the year between our trips.

- As a team, church, or youth group, continue praying for the ministry, the people who are still on the ground serving and reaching their community.

- Connect with the community you served during your short-term mission trip at least once a month, asking how you can pray for them and if they have any tangible needs that you might be able to fulfill.

- Invite them to come to your church if they can, to share and give an update. If they can't make it have them record a greeting to be played.

Leaders Make the Difference

Like all teams, churches, and businesses, leadership is a huge key to success. I have seen short-term mission teams have amazing leaders who are in tune to the community and culture in which they serve, and the trip is a huge success. I have also witnessed leaders who are out of touch and out of tune, not only with the culture they are in but with their team and with God. This type of leadership is devastating to everyone involved.

We have a huge responsibility as a leader of the short-term mission trip to care for our team, facilitating growth and building relationships with those we serve with on the trip. It is our responsibility to be sure that our team knows how to conduct themselves in a different culture. It is our responsibility to be sure that our team knows that we are not bringing God to a community, but riding the river of God's activity already at work. It is our responsibility to engage our church or community in developing a long-term reciprocal relationship with the people we serve with on our short-term mission trip. What an honor that we get to serve and work with people who have given up everything for the sake of the Kingdom of God while on these trips. Let us never take this lightly.

It's a big responsibility, but with planning, God's help, and a solid relationship with your host, it's within reach. And the results will change your team, the community you serve, and you!

DJ's 2 Cents

Leadership matters. This seems obvious, but it's a necessary part to consider in any successful mission trip. The quality and vision of the person leading will make or break the experience. The leader's experience with international work, their vision for the trip, and their ability to share that vision are critical. Beyond the size of the group, beyond anything else, leadership is the single most important part of an effective, impactful mission team.

Define who the leader is. This seems pretty basic, but depending on the team there might be more than a few people who are natural leaders; the team needs to know who is ultimately in charge. Adult teams can be the most challenging—everybody is used to doing things their way, and following directions from someone else can be hard for some people.

Here at our ministry, we coordinate home building projects for needy families in our area. We'll have teams come down to build a wood frame house over the course of a week. If the team has three or four contractors, I make sure they select who is making the ultimate decisions, otherwise they spend hours debating every decision or working in different directions. Your team can come to consensus agreements, but ultimately someone has to say yes or no to any major decision. The leader sets the tone.

Know your team. The maturity, experience, and vision of every team member is a little different. Evaluate your team members to lead them effectively. If your team is under-skilled maybe they shouldn't work on a major construction project; if they're new in their faith, maybe they shouldn't be leading a Bible study or public prayer. If you have a skilled individual (construction, IT, mechanic, etc.) let your hosting organization know that these people are available if needed. Know when to push your team and when to hold them back. Jesus knew His apostles well, their skills, their weaknesses, and their maturity. He knew what they could handle and allowed them to take risks and grow. He also had them wait when needed. You need to be Jesus to your team.

Work on cross-cultural training. If the members of your team have been relatively sheltered and have never been exposed to true poverty or other cultures, coach them in how to respond, react, and process what they're experiencing. Every culture has nuances and differences, but an attitude of mutual respect goes a long way anywhere. Respect for local dress codes, traditions, language, and church culture are all important. Unintentionally offending a culture is a sure way to severely limit a team's effectiveness, both in serving and in ministry.

Everyone has something to learn from others. Americans can carry a fair amount of national pride, and that's OK as long as you realize that other people can be proud of their countries also, even if it isn't America. The "ugly American" stereotype exists for a reason. We need to realize that the culture we're visiting isn't worse than ours, it isn't better than ours, it's different than ours.

Communicate, communicate, communicate. Let your team know the goals, expectations, schedules. Communicate with your team about the importance of flexibility, conflict resolution, and being part of the team. Give your team a written schedule as a guide, knowing things might change. Communicate with your host organization about travel plans, your goals, your skills, and ask them what they would like to receive from your group. From the day you have your dates picked, start communicating with your host organization and ask them everything you can think of. Also let them know everything they might need to know about your team (size of team, ages, skills, any funding available, etc.). You are building a relationship between your team and the team on the ground you will be serving. In any healthy relationship, clear and detailed communication can go along way in avoiding problems or conflicts.

Teach and practice flexibility. When traveling with a team and working in other countries, it's impossible to plan for, or expect, everything. Lost luggage, illness, power outages, can be expected, but sometimes other things come up. I know of a group that was planning on spending a week working on a church building, and the day they arrived a leader from the hosting church died. The project was unexpectedly put on hold, but it did give the team new, unanticipated doors to serve and minister. The change was out of their hands, so they flowed with it correctly, maturely, and with grace.

Lead them into the experience. Mission trips can be overwhelming. Debrief every night, and encourage intentional conversations about what everyone is experiencing. Maybe have everyone turn off the cell phones and focus on the day and the people experiencing the trip with them. It's heartbreaking to see people on a mission trip with so much opportunity, only to watch them stare at their phones the whole time. Lead your team into being intentional and living in the moment. A trip needs to be about more than the perfect Instagram photo.

As a leader, you have a huge responsibility, also a huge privilege. A privilege to lead people into life-changing, mountaintop serving experiences they will remember the rest of their lives. When led and hosted correctly, short-term missions can have world-changing impact. Go and have your world changed.

For most people, the short-term mission trip, or even international travel, is a new experience. As a leader you have a tremendous responsibility to show them the way. If, as a leader, your outlook is healthy and you're serving with a humble, Christ-like attitude, that will set the tone for everyone else on the trip. By doing your homework, through research on your destination and preparation for your goals, you will be more effective. By patiently teaching the team and preparing them before they leave home, you will set them up for success. By guiding them and asking them the right questions while on the trip, you will make it a deeper, more impactful experience. By demonstrating to your team a true servant's heart, your team will have a much greater impact wherever they are serving.

As a leader, you are representing Jesus to your team. Jesus spent a tremendous amount of time in the prayer, preparing for each day. Jesus spent a tremendous amount of time and effort teaching the apostles before He sent them out. When the apostles didn't get it right, Jesus would lovingly guide them to a better attitude and explain how to do it better next time. In short-term missions, as in all areas life, Jesus sets a pretty good example.

CHAPTER 11

Defining
Success or Failure

DJ

Americans like to grade things. Whether it's a child's English class or the type of meat we buy, everybody likes to stamp a grade on it. It makes life so much simpler if we can judge things on a set scale: "This person graduated with a 4.0, this hotel has three stars, this movie got two thumbs up." This works for many areas of our day-to-day lives, but when it comes to relational and spiritual issues, or anything else that is a little harder to quantify, it becomes more complicated. How does one judge the best church service? How does one judge a counseling session? How does one determine what the best hamburger is? It's impossible to say definitively what college gives the best education. Sometimes it's up to the person making the judgment.

When it comes to missions, I've seen people on the same trip give wildly different reports on whether or not it was "successful." So much depends on the person's maturity, their outlook on the trip, and most importantly their expectations and goals.

In this chapter, we're going to look at some of the ways you can quantify whether or not a mission trip or project met, failed, or exceeded the expectations of all those involved—which can be even more challenging when you're focusing on building reciprocal relationships. We won't be able to put a definitive number scale to the trip, but we will look at realistic expectations and, at some level, try to help determine whether a trip worked. Always keep in mind, if you step out in faith and serve the best you can, your trip is a success. We might not know in this lifetime what the impact of a short-term trip is. We can know if we listen to God's instruction to "go out to all the world" and respond accordingly, we've already been successful.

It does help to set up some parameters and at least talk about it. You, and people around you, want to know how your trip went. When a team comes back from a mission trip, it's normal and expected that they would give some kind of report. It might be as formal as presenting about the experience with the church board; it might be having someone share at a Sunday morning service and showing a few slides; it might be answering questions from friends and family that helped to support individuals or the team. People are interested and want to know how people grew spiritually, whether the funds were well spent, and whether they should support future trips.

More importantly than being able to report to others how everything went, evaluating the trip helps you and your team effectively plan for future trips. What went right? What could we have done better? Are we building healthy relationships in our destination country? Were we responsible with the resources we had at our disposal? Was our in-country host someone we want to build an ongoing relationship with? These are all questions that could and should be discussed during the trip, but should definitely be gone over once you get back. By spending time debriefing with the team, or at least the team leadership, it will help you to further anchor the lessons you've learned on the trip and hopefully help you apply those many lessons to your life down the road.

Defining the Goals

At one point a few years ago, I was sent a "missionary survey" by a fairly large church that was sponsoring several missionaries around the world. There is absolutely nothing wrong with asking for information from any missionary or mission the church is supporting; it's part of keeping the relationship going. However, the survey I was sent rubbed me the wrong way because it wasn't focused on relationship. There were about 20 questions that were asking for set numbers, but the questions only brought up further questions:

How many people have you led to Lord of the last six months? Well, is it better to lead to 40 people to the Lord and never speak to them again, or one person and then build an ongoing, healthy mentoring relationship with them while they grow in the Lord?

How many times did you visit homes in your community? Well, does that mean knocking on the door and saying "Hi," or entering in and sitting all day with someone going through a trauma in their lives, helping them to reach a fuller understanding of their walk with God?

How many Bibles did you distribute? Well, what's better: two or three Bibles into people's hands that are excited to have them and will cherish them, or 40 Bibles passed out at swap-meet where they will probably be thrown away?

Aside from the vagueness of the questions, none of what they were asking applied to the work I was doing of running a large orphanage and hosting groups in a majority country. They didn't ask how many children were rescued; they didn't ask how many graduated from high school; they didn't ask how many families we helped to restore. The questions the church sent were only focused on a narrow evangelistic theme. That would have been fine if evangelism was my primary calling (it's not). The survey did not allow for medical missions, orphan care, education, fighting human trafficking, or any one of the dozens of other areas missionaries are frequently involved in.

The point of me sharing about the survey is showing that before you can ask the questions and evaluate your mission trip, it's important to look again at your goals for the team and your goals for serving and blessing others on your trip. If you don't know what your goals were for the trip, you can't possibly know if you reached those goals. If you don't know your ultimate destination, you'll never know if you got there.

Although the goals of most mission trip tend to focus on one area, it is possible, and even healthy, to blend them and let them overlap on any trip. Remember the common kinds of trips discussed in the introduction: evangelistic, construction service, emergency needs, and high skills trips. These are generally the easier ones to quantify. If your goal was to build a house for a low-income family, it's pretty easy to state whether the house was built. If your goal was to deliver emergency supplies or fill an immediate need, it's pretty easy to judge whether you made the delivery. If you were leading or participating in a medical outreach, you could track how many people were treated or how many medical training classes were provided to the community. Where it starts to get more complicated is relationship building on a trip. But relationship is what it's all about.

Looking Beneath the Surface

When done right, short-term missions can have a real and dramatic impact, beyond anything we might imagine—even when it looks like a failure on the surface.

A few years ago we had a group sign up with our organization to build a house in our town through a home-building program that we run. When they signed up, they were sure they would have a large team and all the funding they would need to build a house during their one-week trip. As the trip dates got closer, a few people dropped out, and then a few more dropped out. The funding they were counting on from the people participating dried up as people dropped out. Even after doing a good job of promoting the trip and planning a lot, they were left with six high school girls, one leader, and almost no funding. On paper, from a logical standpoint, this trip was shaping up to be a disaster. In most people's eyes, there were a lot of questions raised: What are six high school girls going to do? What difference can they make? Shouldn't they stay home and use the money more effectively? In spite of the reasonable questions and concerns that were raised, this group strongly felt they were supposed to take this trip. They reached out to us and asked what to do. I told them to come, join our team for a week, and we'd find a way for them to serve.

Once the group arrived, I paired them up with a few local construction guys that I work with. By pairing them with our local team, it accomplished a few things. First, their limited funding was helping provide jobs. Second, they had the privilege of building relationships with people in the community and working side-by-side, both with the family they were helping and the men helping out.

The plan was to help pour a house's cement foundation for a family who'd been on our waiting list for a while, living in a tiny old trailer. This single-child family had a believing wife yet a husband who was more or less the town drunk.

For a week the girls worked very hard alongside my local team. They were there every morning hauling sand, gravel, and doing whatever they could to move the project along. The father could not figure this out. It confused him. A lot. He stood for hours with his arms crossed trying to figure out two things: Why are these odd, blonde American girls helping his family? And why were these local construction guys having such a good time? My local team of guys are all strong believers. They were picking on each other as guys do, flipping wet cement at each other, laughing a lot, and having a blast. They weren't cussing, they weren't drinking, and the father couldn't understand any of this. He had never seen or experienced healthy male relationships before, and he just didn't get it. At no point was the Gospel presented in words, there was no pressure on anyone. This project was just an odd collection of Christians from two cultures serving a needy family. The collective team was putting Christ's love and example of service into action.

The week ended, the girls left, and it might have ended there. But the seeds of Christian service had been planted; the father witnessed Christ's love in action. The following Sunday he was at our local church; the next week he came to the Lord. No one, including him, knew at the time, but he was very sick, and he died about 90 days later. Because this small, unskilled, under-funded team (that didn't speak Spanish) pressed forward; this man is now dancing in heaven.

Before they left, as we debriefed with the team, their reaction was overwhelmingly positive. By the straight evaluation, they couldn't go home and say "we built a house." But they left having completed what we considered a phenomenally successful mission trip. Relationships were built with the local community; relationships were built and made stronger among various team members; and they represented Christ, the church, and our organization incredibly well here in our community. This trip was deemed a success well before we knew that the father in the family would ultimately make a decision for Christ. (I did follow up with the group and let them know about the family.)

Your Project Doesn't Matter—Get Over It

One of the many privileges of hosting hundreds of short-term mission teams over the years is being able to observe the differences in the groups' aptitudes, attitudes, funding, skill sets, and goals—for good or bad.

Without a doubt, our favorite groups are the ones that understand the bigger picture. They come down focused to work on a project and do a quality job, but they realize that the projects themselves are irrelevant. The construction projects, the home builds, and the painting projects are simply tools to build relationships. They understand that we are all in this together and they (or we) do not have everything figured out. Humility goes a long way in mission work.

Reciprocal Missions

When I first started bringing teams to Mexico on weekend trips, I was entirely focused on having our team do a quality construction job for the orphanage where we were serving. I felt like we were making an impact on that orphanage through the construction and painting projects. There is absolutely nothing wrong with that; anything we do for the Kingdom and to serve others should be a quality job. In whatever we do, we are representing Christ and the church.

After I had lead three or four trips, a good friend of mine pulled me aside, and we had a conversation that I remember almost word for word. My friend asked: "In 10 years, will these children remember that we painted the wall? Or will they remember the time we spent with them playing soccer, sharing a meal, and listening to what is going on in their lives?" That one conversation stuck with me and has had a dramatic impact on my ministry over the last 25 years.

Remember in the grand scheme of things—our physical projects are irrelevant to the relationships that we build. The activities we might organize are irrelevant to our heart behind them, and our heart for the people that we are proposing to serve. Does a child care more about a new soccer uniform, or the fact that his parent was present at every game through the season? When a casserole is brought to a grieving family, the quality of the dish might matter, but the fact that an individual would put forth the effort and deliver the meal to the grieving family means so much more. It's all about relationships.

Every year my team host many groups, but we have one group that really stands out. It's a fairly large church from the middle of Iowa. Every year they send large teams into our area, and over the course of two weeks build three to four houses for needy families in our area. If that was all they did that would be plenty—three houses is a huge blessing in our community and a tremendous witness to all those involved in the project, and the surrounding area. But this group from Iowa really gets that it's not about the houses. They go out of their way to build a relationship with the families they are serving. They share meals with the family, and the family usually prepares a few meals for the group. They invite the families to come back with them and spend time around the campfire. Every year when they return, the leaders go around and visit the families that they've met in prior years; sometimes this group even sends packages down for birthdays and graduations for the children in the families. A couple of years ago they took it to another level. They realized that over time they had built about 40 houses. They planned an evening and invited all 40 families to come together for a potluck and games with the kids: it's now an annual event and kind of a big deal in our town.

I, and the many people in the full-time mission field, could not do our work without the groups working on projects and putting up buildings. I like a quality project. But I know that it's just brick, wood, and paint. It's not what is *most* important. Jesus never painted a wall. The Gospels never mention Jesus building a house for someone. Jesus listened. He asked questions. He asked, "What do you seek?" Jesus was (and is) all about relationships.

Evaluating Your Trip

With relationships at heart, here are a few areas to think about and discuss with your team leaders and maybe the team as a whole. Toward the end of a trip or during debriefing are both good times to ask some questions and be ready for honest discussion. Some of the questions put forth cannot be given yes or no answers, but it's still worth talking about.

Were the physical goals of the trip met?
Although building relationships is the goal, projects can be the tools to build those relationships. Whether it was building a house, digging a trench, vaccinating children, or any other activity, the hope is that you at least made some headway in a project, maybe even completed a project, if that was your goal. Doing your best to meet the goal shows your host organization and community that you care about their needs and are true to your word—both key to a good relationship.

Did the receiving host team have everything in order for you to hit the ground running and be as productive as possible?

This is pretty straightforward. In most majority countries it's almost impossible to plan on a tight schedule. There might have been delays in deliveries that were out of control of your hosts. Maybe your host needed the funds you were bringing to start the purchasing process. But if it seems like it was a last-minute, thrown-together project, it might be good to tactfully discuss your concerns with your host.

Was this a truly needed project and impactful for the community and the mission you were there serving?

My guess is that even during the project, whatever it was, you had a gut feeling of whether the project was making an impact or was just busy work for your team. If you felt you were having an impact—great. Rejoice in the fact that your team was able to bless the community and the organization you were working alongside. If you sensed that your project was just busy work to occupy your team, if you want to continue the partnership, consider communicating with your host organization and have a loving, honest conversation. What you might see as busy work, they might see as a critical part of an ongoing project. Sometimes the only difference between digging a trench that has been marked out and building a foundation for a new school or orphanage is how it's communicated. If the team doesn't know the end goal of their project, it's hard to be enthusiastic about it. If, when you're still on the ground, you feel like it's busy work, please talk to your hosts and have them explain the end goal; it's a critical way to motivate your team and show them they are being effective in their efforts.

Were the spiritual goals of the trip met?

Whether the spiritual and relational goals of the trip were met gets a little more subjective, but it's still a good idea to take a look at this and evaluate how things went.

If your team was partnering with a local church, did the members of the congregation or individuals in the room seem receptive and engaged in whatever your team was presenting? I've seen dramas, worship teams, and sermons shared in local churches that would never be let through the door in your average church in the U.S. At the same time, I've seen dramas and worship teams that were astounding, heartfelt, and able to transcend any language difficulties, presenting the Gospel and love of the Lord in powerful ways. Along with the culturally insensitive cliché sermons, I've seen messages shared with a level of transparency and passion that is hard to explain in mere words. Be honest with yourself, do you feel great about what your team presented? Or was it "good enough"? Your host can also provide feedback, with an understanding of cultural elements you might not be aware of.

We had one group coming in that was all set to put on a special service for the kids in our orphanage. I like my kids, and I don't want them to suffer through what some groups bring. I knew this mission group was planning on a few dramas all of my kids had seen before, and my kids would be bored to death. Zero impact. Our kids know the Gospel pretty well, and we have our own programs as a church and as a family. Instead, we had our kids present a program, including worship and a few evangelistic dramas, to the visiting team. It turned out to be wildly successful for both groups. The visiting team was incredibly blessed, and our kids had the opportunity to give back something very special to our visitors. It truly was a reciprocal relationship.

If you want to look beyond numbers—how many people "came forward" or how many Bibles or tracts were handed out—to see more of your long-term spiritual impact, ask for honesty from your hosts and pray they are comfortable enough to be truthful with you.

Were the relationship goals of the trip met?

Relationship goals are different than spiritual goals. They are close, but there is a subtle difference. Did you and your team create new, healthy, reciprocal relationships with people on the ground?

Reciprocal Missions

Did you and your team build deeper relationships with people you've met and worked alongside in prior trips? If you're looking for the long-term spiritual impact, the best way to do that is long-term reciprocal relationships. We are designed to build each other up. If you went on the trip with the right attitude and mindset, you realized that we truly are all equal and have something to learn from each other. Your team might be meeting physical needs, but once again, those physical needs are just a tool to build ongoing healthy relationships if it's done in the right way.

More than anytime in history, ongoing distant relationships are possible. With the advent of the internet and social media, it is possible to stay in contact with and informed about people we meet around the world. (I've been to some of the poorest countries on earth—*everyone* now has a phone.) Once we get past the edited, shiny version of our lives we put out on social media, we can listen to one another and encourage one another from across the globe. Now and then someone will ask me about setting up a pen pal program with the children in our orphanage. Inside I'm saying to myself, *Really? What year are we in?* What I actually tell people is, "Half of my kids are on Facebook now. If they choose to friend you, it's fine." Don't make a contest out of it, but encourage your team to look for ways to build on the beginnings of the relationships that were started during your trip. Relationships are built over time, and a short-term trip can be the beginning of long, fruitful, reciprocal relationships.

Were the educational goals for your team met?

It's OK that you have trips with a goal of educating your team and opening their eyes to a much greater world. If a pastor or leader is honest and spiritually healthy, they want the members of their team to have life-changing experiences. They want members of their team to have their eyes opened to greater spiritual possibilities. They want faith to be both born and renewed through whatever activities are going on. For most people, I believe the spoken reason for a short-term trip is to serve others, but the unspoken reason for the trip is to light a fire under the team that is going and educate them about a bigger world. Speaking from the position of someone who hosts groups, I get this, I encourage this, and it's my prayer that anyone who goes on a short-term trip has a life-changing experience.

The question, "Did the team grow and learn?" is difficult to answer right away, but if the leader does a good job, they will learn before, during, and after the trip. You should be able to see and hear the growth in the team's attitude, the type of questions they are asking, and how they are responding to the questions you are asking. For many people, a week in the mission field is a mountaintop experience they will remember for the rest of their lives.

With many groups I host, at least one person will approach me about coming back for a long-term mission. For me, this is a great indication that the group as a whole was impacted by the trip, and that they found joy in service to others and the newfound relationships they built. There is a hunger for more: more missions, more service opportunities, and more relationships of depth.

Whose Approval Are You Seeking?

Recently our ministry here in Baja was presented with a special opportunity to serve a local need. A family with three children was living in a small camping trailer with a small shed built next to it. Unfortunately, a small fire turned into a large fire and, although they got out safely, the family lost everything they owned. They are not believers; we saw this as an outstanding opportunity to demonstrate God's love.

We normally spend months planning a home build, partnering with groups from the U.S. who help with both funding and labor. The need of this particular family was immediate, so we couldn't follow through with our normal system. We saw it as a wonderful chance for several ministries in our valley to work together to bless this family. At a hastily called meeting with various local ministry leaders, people brought what they could to the table to help this family. One ministry was able to help with some funding; one had some extra doors and windows; several helped with labor. It was inspiring to see everybody step up to help and how the odd mix of ministries worked together. In less than two weeks we were able to build this family a cute little house that was nicer than what had burned down. The body of Christ was working smoothly together to serve those in need. So what could go wrong? Remember, people are messy.

As the teams were finishing as much work on the house as we had resources for, the family realized it wasn't going to be as nice as they expected. No, we weren't going to be able to finish out the shower. No, we weren't going to be able to complete the interior paint. As a group, we had to consider whether we were working for the approval of man or of God? If we're doing it for the approval men, maybe we're the ones bringing the mess to the party.

In missions, as in life, God sees a much bigger panorama. In looking back at the house we built that wasn't appreciated, I can see how God used everything for His purposes. Several organizations got the privilege of working together and sharing with each other. We were called to serve, so we served; that should be plenty. We didn't receive thanks from the family, but we do believe God was pleased. It also led to some great discussions: How often does God pour out His blessings on us, only to have us reject them, complain, or ask for more? More often than not, the results of our efforts are different than we had anticipated.

If we go into any area of our lives with an attitude of empathy, trying to see things from the other person's perspective, we will be more effective. As we approach short-term missions, we need to move past our preconceived ideas of the people we're serving, the needs we think we're addressing, or even why we are going. Go with a plan, but be sensitive and open to simply being present and experiencing God alongside others. Maybe God is sending you to change *you* through the people you'll encounter.

There is a long history of ministry not turning out the way it's expected to. In the Gospel of Luke Jesus healed ten lepers yet only one returned to give thanks and glory to God. Jesus knew that was going to happen; we're not that bright.

The point of all this is that God almost never guarantees the outcome we are expecting or working toward. That's not the plan. God calls us to go and do the will of our Father and represent Him well. Being pleasing to God is more than enough. People likely won't fully appreciate our efforts; they might not say "thank you." The "right" number of people might not come forward at an outreach; the family we build a house for might not be happy with our work. If that bothers us too much, we might need to examine our motivation: Are we doing this for them or for God?

It Comes Down to Blessing

Ultimately, the best way to judge whether a mission trip was successful is if people from both your team and your destination area were blessed before, during, and after the trip. In any healthy relationship, there needs to be profound mutual respect, open lines of communication, and it sincerely needs to be a reciprocal relationship. When the trip is healthy, everybody wins, everyone is blessed, and ongoing healthy relationships have been created.

Phil's 2 Cents

Defining the success of a short-term mission trip can be very difficult. A good question to ask is, "what does a successful reciprocal relationship look like?" Like most new relationships, it will take time to know if you are developing a successful reciprocal relationship. It will be hard to know this on the first trip. Trust and honesty takes time and communication.

Here are a few thoughts on developing a successful reciprocal relationship:

- Did you do unto them as you would have them do unto you? Did you treat them in their community like you would want a group to treat you in your community?

- Are you honoring and respecting the host's house rules while on the trip?

- Are you taking time to get to know who the host leaders are outside of mere trip logistics, like any friendship? What do they like to eat? What do they like to do in their free time (if they get any)? Do they have family?

- Are you communicating with the host community more than just a few times a year?

- Do you know what the host community's needs are throughout the year?

- Are you praying for the host community throughout the year?

Successful reciprocal relationships take time and energy, but are well worth the effort you put into them. Do the work, and the rewards for everyone will have eternal impact.

There are many short-term mission trips that are driven by numbers: how many houses were built, how many decisions were made, how many Bibles were passed out, how many people came to an event. Numbers are not wrong or bad, but they must be put into the right perspective. If we are driven solely by numbers, we can easily begin to see the people we are serving as statistics and not people created in the image of God. Our short-term mission trips will look more like a business than a ministry. It's ok to talk about what you did, but make it secondary to the names you remember and the people you met. Success of a reciprocal mission trip is based on depth and growth of long-term relationships.

CHAPTER 12

Take a Chance

Phil and DJ

Our hope is that the vision of missions we've covered in this book actually brings up more questions than answers. We hope we planted some seeds and inspired you to start or improve a short-term mission relationship. Now it's up to you to explore and grow.

We have been given an incredible opportunity. At no time in history has worldwide travel been as convenient, easy, and affordable. We have skills, resources, and friendships that we are able to share with others. People around the world have experiences, passionate faith, and incredible wisdom that they want to share with us if we are willing to go and listen. We need to do our part of stepping out and taking a chance to go out and improve the lives of others and broaden our own lives at the same time.

We have been commanded to "go into all the world." We serve an incredibly loving God who only wants good things for us and for the people we encounter. God works in such a way that if we step out and trust in Him, all will be blessed. We truly believe that short-term missions blesses all those involved if it's done in the spirit of grace, acceptance, and humility. We are all learning, we are all on the same journey. We come from different cultures, different countries, and different backgrounds, but we share one heavenly Father who wants to bless His children. How great it is that we have this opportunity to fellowship with believers around the world and walk together with them.

Missions is a potluck, as we explored in chapter 5: we all bring something to the table and we all have something to offer. The outcome of any potluck, if everyone participates, is that there will be an abundance for all those in attendance. Everyone who chooses to participate in the potluck can sit down together at a banquet, an all-you-can-eat buffet, where everyone leaves bursting with all they have taken in.

Missions works the same way. If the leadership and the team going have healthy humble attitudes of service and the host organization is walking with a humble attitude of service, everyone wins, everybody leaves the table blessed, satisfied, able to walk more closely with God.

Often as people approach the end of their lives, surveys say they regret not taking more chances. Please do not let this be one of the regrets in your life. Don't be afraid to take a chance. Don't be afraid to fail. Don't be afraid to step out in faith.

Of course, you'll make mistakes. But if we are humble and pursue reciprocal committed relationships, there will be grace and forgiveness from those we are serving. Remember that you are following in a long line of people who took chances, screwed it up, yet learned from their mistakes.

Organizing or participating in a short-term mission trip comes with inherent risks. "What if we don't accomplish our goal? What if something happens to me? What if I lead a trip and it doesn't go well? What if we don't make a difference?" Well, if you don't go, the outcome is pretty clear. But if you take that chance, lives might be changed: your life, the life of your team, and the people you build relationships with around the world.

Reciprocal Missions

"He has shown you, O man, what is good. And what does the Lord require of you but to do justly, and to love kindness and mercy, and to humble yourself and walk humbly with your God?" —Micah 6:8

Endorsements

"Insightful, challenging and life changing..... a must read for those doing short term missions work. DJ and Phil have done a great job of peeling away the layers to get to the heart of mission work by sharing years of experience of what works and what doesn't. It will challenge you to look at how you have been doing things and finding ways to do things in more creative and effective ways. For those just entering the mission field, following their guidance will help you get to the heart of short term missions and avoid many of the pitfalls. When done correctly, it will be life changing for those serving and those being served."

— Dave Hessler, Founder, Life in the Canyon Ministries, Tijuana, Mexico

"Long overdue. This insightful short-term missions book is unlike any other that I have ever read! After forty years of leading and hosting teams, "Reciprocal Missions" changed the way I think about missions. DJ and Phil's vast experience offers team leaders and hosting ministries insights into living their mission relationships more reciprocally, deriving meaningful trips and spiritual growth!"

— Greg Amstutz, Founder, Genesis Diez & Genesis Expeditions, Baja, Mexico

"As the leaders of an international ministry that has hosted hundreds of groups and individuals, Phil and DJ spoke directly to our hearts. Reminding us that God is bringing people to us because He is about to transform their lives forever. It is our privilege to get to be a catalyst for this transformation. This book is a must-read for all missionaries and mission organizations that receive short-term mission groups, as well as all leaders or sending organizations for short-term missions. We can't wait to get this book into the hands of all our partners!"

— Pastors Johnbull and Stacy Omorefe, Co-Founders/Executive Directors City of Refuge Ministries, Ghana.

"Over the past 30 years I have led hundreds of short term teams on mission trips around the world. I've seen the benefit those trips can have on both the team members as well as the host countries and people when they are done right. Sadly, I've also seen the damage that can be done when they aren't done right. DJ and Phil get it right! They present the most comprehensive, strategic and fruitful approach to short term missions I've read. I would say this is required reading for any youth pastor, missions pastor or leader of short term mission teams."

— Glenn Schroder, Regional Coordinator, Vineyard Missions, Mexico & Central America

"Finally a guidebook that helps us as leaders plan our trips and prepare our team members to serve with the focus on things that count for an eternity. We at Club Dust learned we are doing some things right, need to adjust some of what we do and confirmed that short term missions matter! Phil and Dj have shared their experience in an easy to read, inspiring guide for anyone leading groups to serve in Mexico or anywhere in the world. The book will save your group from making the common mistakes that happen when good intentions lead us into other cultures to serve without the focus on things that really count for an eternal change to occur."

— Ray Meltvedt, Founder and President, Club Dust, Baja, Mexico

"Phil and DJ are not writing from a vacuum, they are writing from lived experience among those they serve alongside and learn from. Phil and DJ lay out a clear understanding of how short-term missions can be and is a beautiful life-changing experience. They also show how short-term missions can do damage if not done in a way that honors the local culture, local traditions, local economy and local community. Phil and DJ draw from their vast experience to help us all understand a better way to do short-term missions. If you think short-term missions is a mistake and should not be done, you should read this book. If you are going on a short-term mission trip or considering going on a short-term mission trip, you should read this book. If you are someone who cares about our

Reciprocal Missions

global neighbors, ways we can learn from them and serve alongside them, you should read this book!"

— Matt Krick, Lead Pastor BayMarin Community Church, San Rafael, CA

"Excellent book!!! On any page that you open, this is the living experience of its authors. More than a book, I see it as a powerful manual, highly recommended for anyone who wants to make a difference. If you receive the call to be a missionary, or wish to become involved in missionary trips, this book offers the necessary tools (values, principles and experiences) that you must consider, so that your mission positively impacts those around you. It will help you to give a bigger meaning to your next mission."

— Gabriela O. Velazquez, Executive Director, Genesis Diez, Baja, Mexico

"DJ and Phil have written a must-read guide for anyone involved in short-term missions and cross-cultural volunteer work. Having hosted dozens of volunteer teams during the past several years, we have experienced firsthand the many benefits of healthy short-term missions--and the unfortunate damage caused by uninformed or wrongly-motivated groups. "Reciprocal Missions" tackles these issues head on and provides an excellent template for mutually-beneficial, relationship-building mission trips."

— Brendan and Sarah Mayer, Co-founders, Siloé Ministries
La Mision, Baja, Mexico

"I have worked with both Phil and DJ for the past 12 years on the mission field in Mexico. If anyone has the expertise and knowledge of how to run a superb ministry on the mission field it is DJ; and if anyone has the wisdom and aptitude of how to make short-term missions work, it is Phil. This is the dream team. If you are interested in how short-term missions should be done correctly, this book is for you. Don't discount what a short-term missions trip can do for you, your church, and the ministry where you go to serve. This book is packed with insight from people who have done the "real work" in missions."

— Heidi Elizarraraz, Founder and Executive Director Open Arms Childcare Ministries, La Mision and Camalu Baja Ca, Mexico

"Reciprocal mission experiences? It's about time – and this book is JUST in time. A must read for any missional leader who wants to hear post short-term mission testimonies that are about more than a renewed appreciation for a beautiful home, a soft bed, and roads without potholes."

— Art Greco, Lead Pastor – Outreach, Marin Covenant Church, San Rafael, CA

"Reciprocal Missions is a must read 'guide' for anyone wishing to serve orphanages and needy communities in Mexico, as it provides an insightful perspective from both sides of the equation based on the writers' many years of experience. A clear message in this book is the importance of understanding the culture and the limitations of the community you wish to serve, and to ensure that any projects or assistance you plan to provide is designed to meet the real needs of that community. Sometimes it is best to work through an organization that understands your target community and can guide you as you plan your mission. I appreciate the great insights in this book, and I know that everyone in our organization will benefit from reading it."

— Hilda Pacheco-Taylor, Founder & President, Corazon De Vida, Irvine, California

Reciprocal Missions

"Together, DJ and Phil have over 40 years experience hosting and leading short-term mission groups. They have acquired an unmatched level of knowledge on what does, and does not make a successful team and trip. Not only have they shared what it takes to have a great mission trip, they also meet, head on, the arguments popping up in church circles today against missions in general. What they share in this book should be required reading for mission leaders, their pastors, and anyone thinking about supporting missions"

— Rick VanCleef, Founder and President, Icon Missions,
  Boise, Idaho

"As a long-term missionary who first got my start in missions many years ago with a short term trip to Kenya, I appreciated DJ and Phil's book from start to finish. Now working with many short-term groups and individuals, we see the challenges discussed in these pages and we also see the redemptive path forward. DJ and Phil speak with years of wisdom and experience under their belt, and their words offer such hope for reciprocal relationships between on-the-ground organizations and their volunteers. As someone who helps to oversee hundreds of volunteers each year with our organization, this will be a book that we will recommend to everyone who passes through our doors. Filled with challenging insights, a sense of humor, and biblical truth, DJ and Phil carefully lay out how to build healthy, life-giving, Christ-centered, reciprocal relationships that will help shape and grow both the volunteers that visit and us as an organization."

— Autumn Buzzell, Director of Education, City of Refuge Ministries,
Ghana

"You're still here? It's over. Go home. Go!"

— Ferris Bueller, Glenbrook North High School, Northbrook, Il.